What in the World?!

What in the World?!

A Southern Woman's Guide to

Laughing at Life's Unexpected Curveballs

and Beautiful Blessings

Leanne Morgan

CONVERGENT

NEW YORK

Published in the United States by Convergent Books, an imprint of Random House, a division of Penguin Random House LLC, New York.

CONVERGENT BOOKS is a registered trademark and the Convergent colophon is a trademark of Penguin Random House LLC.

LIBRARY OF CONGRESS CATALOGING-IN-PUBLICATION DATA
Names: Morgan, Leanne, 1965– author.
Title: What in the world / Leanne Morgan.
Description: First edition. | New York : Convergent, 2024. |
Identifiers: LCCN 2024016303 (print) | LCCN 2024016304 (ebook) |
ISBN 9780593594391 (hardcover) | ISBN 9780593594407 (ebook)
Subjects: LCSH: Morgan, Leanne, 1965– |
Comedians—United States—Biography.
Classification: LCC PN2287.M699755 A3 2024 (print) |
LCC PN2287.M699755 (ebook) |
DDC 792.702/80924 [B]—dc23/eng/20240416
LC record available at https://lccn.loc.gov/2024016303
LC ebook record available at https://lccn.loc.gov/2024016304

Printed in the United States of America on acid-free paper

convergentbooks.com

2 4 6 8 9 7 5 3 1

First Edition

Book design by Caroline Cunningham

To Jimmy, Lucille, Chuck, Charlie, Maggie,

Tess, C.W., and J.J., the reason for everything

CONTENTS

What in the World?!
I Wrote a Book!

It seems hard to believe. I graduated from the sweetest little high school in a rural area. We didn't know what marijuana was, but we couldn't write a paper either. Instead of chemistry or a foreign language, I took home economics. I learned how to flip an omelet, and just like that, I graduated. And now I've filled hundreds of pages with stories about my life that are going to throw you for a loop. You might want to pour yourself a Diet Coke and open a box of cheese straws before you read on. Okay! Let's have a ball, shall we?

Since you picked this book up, you probably know some things about me. Like the fact that I am a southern girl who loves babies and dogs and likes to kiss them both on the mouth. I have a husband who doesn't chat, which is good because I talk enough for the both of us.

You might've seen me on a comedy tour, like Just Getting Started or the Big Panty Tour. Or you might've heard a sweet lady call me "Mrs. Maisel of Appalachia" on NPR. You might even be one of the dolls who threw a pair of Sam's Club panties at me onstage. Is there a more beautiful sight than thousands of darling, fun women laughing so hard they wee-wee themselves? Who would have thought so much joy would come from women pee-peeing? It is a privilege I do not take for granted. For that matter, who would have thought a woman who focused on being a mama through her twenties, thirties, and forties would perform at the Grand Ole Opry and have a Netflix special in her midfifties?

My comedy isn't about all that, though. For instance, I talk about what's really going on with my stomach. It looks like a small purse. When you write to me on social media and say "I'm living your life," I know it's true. If we met in person, we could have a ball talking about recipes, hot flashes, and all the diets we failed at. All I can do with this crazy late-in-life success in comedy is soak it in, wipe away a stray tear, and think, *What in the world have I done to deserve this?*

Every day, I pinch myself. Every day, I'm amazed. For decades, I felt so unseen in the comedy industry, and now I have enough fans out there to get a major publisher to sell my book. How is it even possible? Nobody expected this to happen. Growing up, I didn't know a soul in the entertainment business and never even took so much as a dance class. I didn't perform in a comedy club until I'd had three babies and was in my thirties. When I got onstage, I wasn't in black leather, making jokes about taking mushrooms, shaving B-A-L-L-S (I'm spell-cussing while you're reading this), or, dare I say, F-E-L-L-A-T-I-O. I was in a kitten heel and capri pant with birds on them, talking about raising my kids and loose doo-doo balls in the grocery store—and it didn't always go over well. A lot of people in clubs were drunk and high, and let me tell you, they didn't want to hear about birthing, breastfeeding, or T-ball. But you precious readers heard me and felt like I was talking about your own lives. I became the rarest of gems: a fifty-five-year-old woman from rural Tennessee, with a spray tan and jeans with some stretch in them, who people wanted to come out to see.

The reason this has all happened to me is because of y'all. You found me, and now I hope this book finds you.

The stories in *What in the World?!* are about being a woman, a daughter, a mother, and a wife and finding my own voice after so many years of trying to figure out what in the world that even means. Through good times (like earning a college degree, getting married, and landing a TV deal) and bad times (like dropping out of college, getting divorced, and watching my TV deal disappear before my eyes), God was always with me to show me a door, either the way out of a tough situation or the way into something better.

I've ridden the roller coaster, sometimes loving it and sometimes screaming to get off. Whenever I was kicked in the teeth by life, people would talk about the silver lining, and I'd say, "I don't see it! Are you crazy?" It took me a long time to figure out that I needed to be grateful for the valleys because God had me there for a reason. What I learned sustained me until the next mountaintop, and hallelujah, it gave me great stories to tell.

My overriding "What in the world?" amazement about where I am now is that all the hard times I faced in the past suddenly make perfect sense to me. God's presence in everything I have gone through up to this point is so evident. I have tears running down my face as I write this. We've all had joy and heartbreak. We've all had ups and downs. I've survived mine by trying to find the funny in every situation and, eventually, having the faith that things will sort themselves out. It might take a while, but in the end, everything's going to be all right. Every time you find yourself saying "What in the world?" you're one step closer to getting where you want to go.

What in the World?!

CHAPTER 1

Meet the Fletchers

The thing about families is that, growing up, you think yours is just like everyone else's because it's all you know. As an adult, you look back and think, *Whoa, we were so not normal.*

I always knew as a child that the Fletchers were not normal for Adams, Tennessee, where I grew up. It wasn't until later that I realized we weren't normal for *anywhere*.

Adams is a town of approximately five hundred people. It is so close to the northern border that if you threw a piece of fried chicken as hard as you could, you might hit Kentucky (best fried chicken in the world!). In Adams, most everyone was the same. They had the same houses, farms, clothes, attitudes, everything.

My family was just like the rest in some ways. I came from farming people on both sides. We didn't live in a mansion or anything. Our house was a 1,400-square-foot ranch with three bedrooms, a kitchen, a living room, and one and a half bathrooms. All the land around us was grazed on by cows, horses, pigs, and mules. We were always driving slow behind tractors and combines and waving to everyone as we went by.

But we were different in other ways that, in my mind, made us special.

WE HAD OUR OWN COCA-COLA MACHINE

The biggest thing that set my family apart from all the farmers in Adams was that the Fletchers were also business owners. My daddy, Jimmy Fletcher, ran the only grocery store for twenty miles. The store was like our family's stage, where everyone in town came to hang out and visit with us and watch us work. Daddy had learned amazing butcher skills at a previous job at Kroger, and people loved how he cut up meat. Then he'd wrap it up pretty in butcher paper and tape like a Christmas present.

My mama, Lucille, worked part-time at the cash register and had a ball talking to everyone while smoking a Winston Light, drinking a Tab, and occasionally wearing a hairpiece that made her look like Brigitte Bardot. I wasn't the only one who thought she was the most glamorous woman in Adams.

And then there was me, Little Miss Early Talker. By the time I was in kindergarten, Mama would prop me up on the counter by the cash register and call the customers to gather round to listen to whatever came out of my mouth.

"Leanne, tell them your favorite flavor of ice cream," she said.

I didn't need prompting. I held court to half a dozen farmers, mama's friends, and a clutch of grandmas about the virtues of chocolate, vanilla, and strawberry. And then the punch line: "But I love pinto beans too!" Everyone laughed, and then they went back to chewing tobacco and squeezing tomatoes. People might have come for our Coca-Cola machine, but they stayed for the wit.

On Mondays, the new supplies came in. My sister, Beth, and I helped stock the shelves. I thought of this as a big responsibility. I'm sure I was no help at all. I would work a little and then, while drinking a Tab (just like Mama), I'd take the cans of Lysol and spray them until they were empty. My parents would yell, "Leanne, quit spraying the Lysol!" I could have killed myself from inhaling all those chemicals, but the place smelled fresh.

The only other hot spot in town that rivaled ours in popularity was the funeral home. (Did I mention there weren't many things to do in Adams? We had one caution light.) We'd walk past it on the way to the grocery every day. Mama would peek in, and if she saw people inside, she'd say, "Someone's in the funeral home! Let's see who's in there." We wound up going to a lot of funerals. It wasn't a morbid hobby. Everyone in Adams was practically kin, and going to a funeral was a social occasion when there wasn't much else going on. We'd just visit. It felt normal to me, nothing to be scared of. And afterward there was a big meal, which meant fried chicken and deviled eggs. I was not complaining.

MAMA TRULY BELIEVED THE SUN SHONE OUT OF MY BUTT

I thought I was special because my mama told me I was, every single day.

"You are so *funny*, Leanne," Mom said. "Everyone loves listening to you talk big."

As a little child, I had a lot of very important things to say, like telling people how to ride a bike or how much fun I had at the Shrine Circus. That confidence was spoken into me by Lucille. She always built me up. According to her, I was the funniest, prettiest, and smartest child in town. I wasn't an idiot compared to the other kids, but the smartest? Really? Mama genuinely thought that about me, but let's face it, she was blowing smoke up my butt. (She still does.)

My sister, Beth, three years older than me, was painfully shy and introverted and would have rather died than draw attention to herself. Beth grew up to be five foot ten and strong enough to lift a mattress with her head and dust under it. But as a child, she was skinny and frail. She refused to eat anything but Red Hots, SweeTarts, and steak, a diet that made her get dizzy and faint in the canned food aisle at the store at least twice. Daddy pestered her about eating and nagged her to be as hearty as me. "Beth, look at Leanne eat," he'd say. "She *likes* pinto beans."

I wonder if I became more extroverted to compensate for Beth's shyness. If I entertained people to take the spotlight off her. That's right. My being the center of attention was really an act of selfless kindness toward my sister.

THE SPOTLIGHT SEEMED TO FOLLOW ME AROUND

Wherever we went, Mama and I drew attention. One time, she took Beth and me to the mall in Nashville for an Easter egg hunt. I was six. A photographer was taking pictures for a big newspaper. Out of all the little children, he zeroed in on me and asked me to pose. He didn't have to tell me what to do. I knew to smile and hold it. I took a big bite out of my cupcake and held that pose too. I knew to press my stuffed bunny against my face, all the while thinking, *He needs this shot.* None of the other kids were paying attention. He wasn't going to get anything out of them. But I hammed it up, smiled real big, and did a few twirls. *This will look great in the paper.* I just knew it.

Afterward, I went over to Mama, who was talking with the

other moms nearby. "Why did that photographer take my picture and not anyone else's?" I asked.

She said, "Baby, you stand out. You have a spark."

That pattern repeated itself in other scenarios. If there was a magician at a birthday party, he would have me pick a card. This didn't happen once or twice. It happened every single time. When the blackboard needed cleaning in kindergarten, the teacher *always* handed the eraser to me. I didn't ask for it, but I got it anyway. Teachers were constantly pulling me up to the front of the class to make announcements, and I did it with gusto. I wonder whether I had a look on my face that said, *Please pick me. I'm a ham. You won't be disappointed.*

I got even more attention from my extended family. When children have people around who love them, it builds confidence. By doting on me, my great-aunts made me feel special. They drove me around after school to the Revco pharmacy to pick up their Tums and prescriptions, and they let me order fries and a milkshake at the counter. (Lord, I love a drugstore. You have to drag me out of CVS.) They took me to the hair salon every week to show me off. The salon ladies would put rollers in my hair and park me under a big hair dryer. I'd sit there, sipping a Coke, wearing big black sunglasses, looking and feeling like a mini movie star.

OTHER KIDS DREAMED OF BEING ROCK STARS; I DREAMED OF SELLING CLOROX

Actually, most of the girls I grew up with went on to marry local boys who farmed and ended up having babies. I kind of wanted that too, but I knew in my heart that my life was going to be different from everyone else's, even though I was just a country girl from the middle of nowhere. I could make people laugh. I was cute. And I believed I was going to leave Adams one day, go out into the world, and do *something big*.

The only person I shared these thoughts with was Lucille. She would say, "You are going to be a star. You're going to be like Marilyn Monroe. You photograph well because you've got blond hair on your body. That helps in Hollywood." *What?* I believed her!

My uncle Raymond had other ideas. "You should take over for Vanna White," he said. (It's incredible she's still doing it!) "You're blond and you could turn those letters and smile real big." Just the thought made me smile. *He's right. I could be Vanna White.* (I wouldn't take that job now, unless I wore a good orthopedic. She has really kept her weight down.) I could have been a *Price Is Right* girl too, with the right hair and makeup and my fast metabolism back then. Or I could have made jokes from the center square like Paul Lynde from *Hollywood Squares*, which Mama and I watched obsessively. If my mother and uncle thought I could be a game show star, it had to be true.

I needed to prepare for my future on TV, so I practiced being a spokesmodel for commercials in the mirror. *When I'm famous, Clorox is going to want me to go on TV and talk about their bleach,* I thought. I took to mixing Drano and Pine-Sol, whatever I could find under the sink, to create the ultimate product to pitch in future commercials. My concoctions smelled like Chernobyl. If I got too close to them, I felt dizzy. I didn't know not to mix chemicals in a closed room. It's a wonder I didn't poison myself. Nothing in the house was off-limits. I'd grab a bottle of Hershey's chocolate syrup, the vacuum, or Lucille's good lipstick, hold it close to my face in the mirror, and brag on it. Hours would go by.

Preparing for my future stardom was more fun than other

games I made up, like throwing a corn kernel down the drain and waiting for a stalk to grow three days later.

I still did that too, though, because I liked to stay busy.

MY FIRST PERFORMANCE

At age seven or eight, I said to Lucille, "I want to be like Joey Heatherton on the Jerry Lewis telethon and tap-dance in black tights."

She said, "I'm so sorry, my baby, I would love to get you dance lessons, but there's nowhere to go." The closest place was forty-five minutes away in Nashville, and Mama didn't drive until she was in her forties.

"That's okay, Mama. I'll just tap here."

I rolled up a corner of the living room rug and stomped the floor to death. I had no idea what I was doing, but I made a lot of noise, and I loved it.

My real dream was to perform in front of actual people. Opportunity knocked, literally, when an insurance man came to the house to sell my parents a policy. He looked like Glen Campbell, but not as jazzy, in navy polyester Sansabelt pants, a white shirt with a pocket calendar, and sideburns. I had no idea who he was or why he was sitting on our couch. But he'd spread out a bunch of papers on the table and accepted Mama's offer for coffee. He wasn't going anywhere for a while.

I'm going to tap for this man, I thought.

I ran to my room and put on my Sunday shoes—black patent leather Mary Janes. They didn't have metal tips and heels like real tap shoes, but they were still pretty loud. I dashed back to the living room and said, "Hello. I'm Leanne, and I'm going to do a little dance for you."

He looked super uncomfortable and glanced around for Mama. She was nowhere in sight, so he smiled weakly at me and said, "Well, aren't you sweet?"

That was my cue. This was a big opportunity, and I wasn't going to let it pass me by. For the next ten minutes, I proceeded to pound the floor with my little feet and flap my arms. I gave it everything I had, convinced he was loving it. (I hadn't learned to read a room yet.)

Daddy yelled from the kitchen, "Leanne, don't scar up the hardwood!"

I finished big with a stomp, a twirl, and a "ta-da!" This man had a terrible look on his face, which I mistook for awe. He clapped slowly, smiled at me, and said, "That was just great, sweetheart." Proof of my skills! I was thrilled.

It never occurred to me that he might've put up with me to butter up Mama so she'd buy a policy. I took his praise as real and genuine. It was a clear sign that I had a future in showbiz.

HAMMING IT UP FOR REAL

When I was twelve, Daddy sold the grocery store and built a meat processing facility on the hill behind our house. It made sense to my father. At the store, people were so dazzled by his custom butchery that they wouldn't leave him alone about cutting up their cows and hogs. He wasn't making much money running the store anyway because people would charge their groceries and wait for the crop to come in to pay their bill. By then, Kroger and other big grocery stores were around, and people drove twenty minutes to buy their groceries there. He saw a need that wasn't being met and thought, *I'm going to cut up customers' meat full-time.*

When Daddy asked family and friends about his idea, they

all said something like, "Jimmy Fletcher, you won't have enough business. You'll never make a living at that." I know my dad is special because even though everyone thought his plan would be a disaster, he did it anyway.

He built the meat processing building himself out of cinder blocks. It had two rooms. The bigger room had two massive freezers, stainless steel tables, sinks, and tools for cutting, wrapping, and freezing meat. The smaller room was the office, which had a bathroom and the Coca-Cola machine we kept from the store.

Daddy took out a twelve-dollar ad in the local paper to announce Fletcher's Meat Processing, and he got so much business from it that he never had to advertise again. Back then, custom butchering was rare (pun intended). As soon as people found out about Daddy's business through word of mouth, it was on like Donkey Kong. We were up to our eyeballs in sides of beef, deer, and pork.

The way my parents ran the business—as equal partners—wasn't normal in 1978. Mama worked full-time at Fletcher's Meat Processing, and I was so proud of that. Her main jobs were doing the books, wrapping the meat, and taking orders from customers over the phone. Lucille could have been a therapist. People would come to pick up their meat, and if she gave them one compassionate look, they'd start unloading every awful thing that had ever happened to them. She's a wonderful listener and everyone loved her. It was always like that. Most Sundays, we couldn't get out of the church parking lot because people surrounded her to tell her their problems. And she dazzled. I would watch her in awe. To me, she was so beautiful, like a movie star. She could bring home the bacon and fry it up in a pan. Plus, she helped butcher it too.

Our busiest time of year for meat processing was Thanksgiving, the start of deer hunting season. Deer were easier to butcher than cows because they were smaller, but good night, were they sticky. People would bring their field-dressed deer straight to us from the woods with the heart, guts, and head removed. We would get so many, we couldn't process them fast enough. We had to hang them from trees in our yard until it was their turn. If you were looking for my house at that time, all you had to do was keep your eyes peeled for the swinging carcasses.

We didn't have a normal Thanksgiving dinner for twenty years. Everyone in our family, plus our friends and some teenage boys we hired to help, pitched in to process the deer as quickly as possible. We lined up along the stainless steel tables wearing rubber gloves, flannel shirts, and toboggan hats. The men helped Daddy with the butchering, and the women, including Beth and me, did the wrapping and labeling. The hired boys thought it was hilarious to mess with me by throwing a kidney or a piece of liver at my head. The funny thing is I think they were flirting with me. (My teenage concept of courtship was definitely skewed.)

They'd hang a deer outside on a pulley, and my super feminine mother with her hairpiece and good lipstick would tuck a golf ball under the hide on the back of the neck, tie a rope around the golf ball, and then pull the rope to peel the skin off the entire deer, like yanking down a sock, in two minutes flat. It was really something to see. I didn't love the squishy, ripping sounds myself, but our customers, granddaddies, aunts, hunters, workers, everyone who happened to be there, would sit on chairs on the grass and watch her do it. We could have sold tickets.

December was hog-killing time. I'm going to spare you the gory details about what happens when you butcher a hog. I've seen it. It traumatized me. Trust me, you do not want to know.

Daddy hired a man, Mr. Gower, to go to customers' farms, slaughter their livestock, and bring the animals back for processing. Mr. Gower had only seven fingers, which fascinated me. How did he wear gloves? How did he hold a fork? He answered all my questions, however annoying. He was just a doll.

So many cuts come off a hog, and we spent countless hours wrapping roasts and ribs. It was not nearly as fun as wrapping Christmas presents. We had a giant grinder at the building to process the trimmings into Mama's famous smoked sausage. People said, "Lucille's sausage is so good, it makes you want to smack somebody." We should have printed that on the labels. The recipe is a Fletcher family secret, but here's a taste: The spice mix included salt, red pepper (hot or mild), and special sage that Mom ordered from Canada. The meat and spices went into the grinder together. The mixture that came out was put into cloth sacks, two pounds apiece, that we tied with twine. Then the sacks were hung over smoldering wood chips in a smokehouse for days. People tried to copy her recipe, but they never could. As a child, I was so turned off by meat that I became a vegetarian for a few years, but I was still tempted to eat that sausage. That says a lot.

Some of our customers were celebrities, like farm girl Pat Summitt, the famous women's basketball coach for the University of Tennessee. The president of the Grand Ole Opry placed orders with us too and sometimes sent us free concert tickets. I got to see a sold-out Dolly Parton and Porter Wagoner concert that way. I was never told when the people from the Grand Ole Opry were coming. My parents knew I would have put on my tap shoes and tried to bust a move for them.

Unlike most homes in Adams, where people cherished their peace and quiet, ours was a buzzing gathering place. Picture a few old men standing around eating peanuts outside, Mama in her office counseling a poor woman whose husband just ran off, and Beau, the fat stray beagle, sitting in the middle of the yard with a cow leg in his mouth. I was always part of the action, but Beth stayed inside reading *Seventeen* magazines and making scrapbooks about *Charlie's Angels* hairstyles.

THE MOST UNIQUE AND SPECIAL THING ABOUT THE FLETCHERS

The most unique thing about my home was the smell. It was the one major drawback to living near a meat processing plant. Lord, it was horrible, like sage-infused death. Over time, I got used to it and didn't notice. But it was everywhere: in the air, in my hair, and in my clothes. When Daddy built the plant, he decided not to install a washer and dryer there to clean the bloody aprons and rags. It would have cost another chunk of change, and he was so worried about money. "We can wash the aprons back at the house," he said.

So Mama threw the aprons into the same machines we used for our regular clothes. She tried to keep the loads separate, but sometimes a pair of underwear would get mixed in with the aprons. Eventually, the smell was in the machine itself, and everything that went into it came out revolting. All my clothes stank of meat.

It didn't help that our one house dog, a Peekapoo named Honey, was my best friend. His breath was terrible, but I kissed him on the mouth and held him like a baby anyway. That's what love is. His wet dog aroma clung to me too.

When I was in seventh grade, my meaty scent wasn't helping me achieve my junior high goal: to dazzle. I hoped to do that by being funny and good at sports and just leaning into being a Fletcher. Fortunately, most of my classmates worked on farms with manure and compost, and they didn't smell like French perfume either. We sort of canceled each other out.

In health class, one of the basketball coaches was doing a lecture on nutrition. He said, "Y'all need to eat protein. Good sources of protein are pork and beef." Every kid in the class turned to look at me. They knew about our business; their families were our customers. Most teenage girls might be offended by or feel insecure about being associated with the words "pork" and "beef." But I wouldn't have minded if my junior high nickname was "grade A prime." I was proud of our family's success, proud of my risk-taking daddy, proud to have a working mother I looked up to. I sat up straighter in my chair whenever Fletcher's Meat Processing came up. It was just one more thing about my family that made me feel special.

On the other hand, whenever I sat in a closed classroom on a hot day, my uniquely bad odor got worse. Someone would inevitably start sniffing the air and say, "What is that *smell*?"

Good thing I was cute and fun, or everyone would have steered clear!

My Big Break That Never Happened

Every year, Adams threw a big Fourth of July picnic, and every few years, the picnic included a talent show. We'd gone to see it as a family a couple of times, and frankly, I was not impressed by the juggling acts and the ventriloquist. You could see his lips moving from the back row.

The summer I was nine, the talent show was back on, and I was going to shake it up. *I have to perform at the talent show because, Lord, these people need me*, I thought. I owed it to the citizens of Adams to dance a little and be funny. My loose plan was to bring my portable record player onstage with me, play "Half-Breed" by Cher, and do a tap number with Native American dance moves that would not have aged well.

In the days leading up to the picnic, I pictured myself walking onto center stage in complete silence. The people would perk up when they heard the music. After I did my thing, they'd cheer and hoot while I took dainty bows and said, "Thank you. You are all too kind." Just imagining my triumph felt *right*. It felt inevitable.

Still, I didn't tell my parents or Beth what I had planned. I hadn't studied dance. I was winging it. Even though I believed I'd kill, I'd never done this before, and a tiny part of me thought I might embarrass them. The night before, I prayed about whether I should go through with it. God told me clear as day that performing was what I was meant to be doing. Not only was it my destiny to entertain these people, but I just knew I was going to win the whole thing.

As the time for the talent show drew near, I mentally prepared to blow the roof off the high school gym. But a few minutes before it started, Beth and my parents found me backstage, and they didn't look happy.

Mama said, "Leanne, Beth told us you signed up for the talent show."

"I bet she's going to sing that Cher song and dance around like an idiot!" shouted Beth. "I'll be humiliated!" And then she started bawling.

"You've just got to let me go on," I pleaded to my parents. "*I'm going to win this thing.*"

I could see the conflict in their eyes. They didn't want to upset either one of us. Lucille would sooner die than discourage me. And Daddy was so bighearted, it pained him to disappoint anyone. But when Beth started crying, my parents were helpless. We all lived in fear of frail, weak Beth collapsing. It was a hot day. They just couldn't take the risk.

"I'm so sorry, Leanne," said Mama. "We can't let you go on."

I was *devastated,* and furious. My stage debut was canceled. It was my time to shine, and Beth ruined it! When would I get another chance? I decided I would never, ever, not under threat of death, speak to my sister again.

During the ride home, I was too mad to talk, which was a first. Beth really felt it. She woke me up at dawn the next day, crying, and apologized. Of course, I forgave her, frail slip of a thing that she was. And I vowed it was the last time I would let anyone stop me from going on a stage again.

To this day, Beth brings up that talent show every two or three months. I have to say, "Good Lord, Beth. Let it go!"

It took fifty years to get to whatever level of stardom I'm at, which was a bit longer than I thought. But that was God's timing too. The fact is, Beth's blocking me that day might have saved my life. If my "Half-Breed" catapulted me to child stardom, as I thought it would, I'd probably be in rehab or dead by now. So in a way, I'm grateful to her for that.

CHAPTER 2

Being So Cute

In the South, girls of my generation were expected to be pretty to find a good husband. Being funny and smart was good too, just as long as it didn't scare off a man.

In high school in my small-town culture, getting married and having children were prioritized over pursuing higher education, which might explain why I didn't do well in algebra. I never got the basics on how to write an English paper either, but I learned how to make Baked Alaska and hold a baby (which I loved) in home economics. Instead of taking chemistry, I took sewing and made a groovy pair of jodhpurs that tragically fell apart in the wash.

Lucille was the brains behind our family business, but she embraced the southern custom of enjoying prettiness. It didn't mean she was shallow. She wanted us to be educated and go to college, but being attractive was good too. "Things are just easier for pretty people," she said. Good looks earned you compliments and boosted your self-esteem, and, one day, they would land you a husband with health insurance.

She was only preaching what she'd been taught by her mama and generations of southern women before her. Lucille is a Richards, and they are very pretty people, with smooth, creamy skin and thick, wavy hair. Any one of her cousins could have been a spokesmodel on *The Price Is Right.*

Of course, I thought Lucille was the prettiest by far. And I loved to watch her primp. On Saturday mornings, I sat on the edge of the bathtub and watched her roll up her hair into Velcro rollers and douse it with hairspray. She'd leave it like that for the whole day and then take out the rollers for Saturday night. After finishing her makeup, she'd look at herself in the mirror and say, "I am *so pretty!*" She knew that would get a giggle out of me.

Beauty wasn't my top priority, but I was glad to have a little bit of it, especially when it was so important to those around me. I learned a few things about the power of pretty that helped me get through life.

CUTE AND FUN CAN MAKE PEOPLE FEEL GOOD

At fifteen, my goal was to dazzle with my personality more than my looks. I used my wit and charm in class by reading the room and making sure no one felt left out. If someone was sitting alone, I'd say, "Hello, darling! Come sit by me and let's talk about a whole bunch of nothing." I can't do math. I've got many flaws. But I can tell if someone needs attention, and I can make people laugh. Everyone has gifts, and those are mine.

I spent the rest of my efforts on the court and field. I joined every team: volleyball, basketball, and softball. Cheerleading was for people with spirit. I have *some* spirit, but I wanted to play ball. Basketball was my favorite. My coaches thought I talked too much, but they liked me because I took the game seriously, I got the crowd involved (thank you, spark), and I thought I was so fun to watch with my long blond ponytail whipping through the air.

My coach once suggested I gain twenty-five pounds over the summer so I could box out better under the goal. I actually wanted to do it. That was how serious I was about the sport. But my daddy said, "No, Leanne, you are not doing that! That's crazy." He was right. I wasn't going to be a college athlete, so why would I bulk up? I mean, I was good. But I wasn't *that* good.

I don't know if it would have even been possible. My metabolism at fifteen was like a rabbit's. I didn't know how good I had it! As a grown woman, I did Weight Watchers nine times, and I lost a total of seven pounds. I would eat all my food points before noon. I kept trying to beat the system, thinking, *You're not going to keep me in those points. I'm going to run ten miles to eat Little Debbie Swiss Rolls!* It was stupid! I dreaded those weigh-ins. Gaining weight made me feel so bad, I'd go straight home and eat a sleeve of Oreos in a closet. I compensated by flirting with the weigh-in volunteer, a little elderly man named Ed who took my eleven dollars each week.

More times than I'd care to admit, as I stepped on the scale, I'd say, "Ed, I had a terrible week. My friends sabotaged me with Dove chocolates."

He'd say, "Don't worry about it, girl. We just won't do it this week." And then he'd write the number on my little card and give me back my money.

"Thank you, doll! Let's go to Cracker Barrel after."

Would Ed have been so nice to me if I weren't sweet? I don't know. We had a bond. He was so tickled when he saw me that he'd smile so big I could see his tonsils.

IT'S HARD TO GET THAT '80S LOOK

Even for those of us born lucky, you can't just assume being pretty is a sure thing. You do have to work at it, I learned.

My sister was obsessed with makeup. I didn't wear any until Beth convinced me to try some of her Merle Norman lipstick. I applied it, looking in the mirror, and it was like I'd seen the light. Like Mom, I said out loud, "I am *so pretty!*" From that day on, I was really into beauty products. Beth and I bonded over it. We would go to the Merle Norman store in Springfield to get free makeup consultations. I also started using spongy foam rollers on my hair. The way they worked was that you twisted a lock of hair around the foam roller and put a clip on it. Then you slept in them and took your hair out right before school. Oh my gosh, they did *not* make a pretty curl. Beth and I called them "doo-doo curls" because they were so tight and little. We had a head full of doo-doo!

One afternoon, I was walking down the school hallway with way too much eyeliner and doo-doo curls, feeling prettier than the Tomato Queen of Grainger County. My basketball coach was walking toward me from the other direction. When he saw me, he did a double take. He didn't say a word, but his body language and the look in his eyes said, *It's over. Leanne doesn't care about basketball anymore.*

And he was right. I went from being a sports-obsessed tomboy to being someone who said, "I've got to put my face on." Before, I would beg to play in every minute of the games. After, I was happy to sit on the bench, cut up, and have a good time. I was still a starter, but I didn't care if we won or lost. I worried about making my teammates laugh and keeping my hair from wilting on the court.

Wisely, I upgraded from foam to hot rollers for a softer curl.

The best thing about hot rollers was that they set in an hour. If my curls didn't turn out the way I wanted them to, I could wash my hair and start over. Beth did the same. The man who ran the water plant in Adams told Daddy that our family used more water than any other household in the entire town. And I know it was because my sister and I were in the shower multiple times a day. We spent much more time on our hair than we ever did on studying. I regret that now. When my daughter Maggie was little, she would ask me about the solar system, like, "How many planets are there?" and "What's a black hole?" A black hole? Isn't that just a really deep pothole? I said, "I don't know, but if you have any questions about *The Young and the Restless*, I've got you."

If I had paid more attention to my studies than my hair, I probably wouldn't be a comedian. So maybe that's a good thing.

When it looked perfect, my mane was teased on the top and sides and curled at the bottom. It added three inches to my height, which made me fearsome on the basketball court. On game day, I teased my hair way up and wore tons of makeup. At tip-off, I was pageant ready. We didn't have waterproof mascara back then, unfortunately. By the end of a game, I looked like Tammy Wynette and Alice Cooper had a child together.

Meanwhile, Beth strutted her stuff on the football field, twirling the baton in the marching band. Mama had tricks for making Beth stand out as the prettiest majorette. She wore a tight panty under her uniform that kept her tummy even flatter than it was, and Mama pulled up the sides of the uniform to make Beth's extremely long legs look longer. Meanwhile, all the other mothers were pulling their daughters' uniforms down to be more modest, which made their legs look stumpy. I don't know whether Beth was the best twirler on the squad, but it didn't matter. She stood out.

One week my sister got her picture in the paper in her majorette outfit. All of a sudden, boys started calling the house and breathing into the phone. No one does that anymore. Nowadays, they just text a nasty eggplant. I hate to even say that out of my lips.

CUTE AND DAZZLING GETS YOU HONKED AT

People called Beth and me "the Fletcher girls." Tall, slim, and blond, we would cover ourselves in baby oil and lie out in bikinis on foldout chairs in the backyard where there were snakes. If a truck driver saw us from the road, he would honk his horn. We didn't think it was rude. We were flattered by it.

We thought we were such a big deal, walking down the street like we left a trail of glitter dust behind us. Looking back, I'm sure people thought, *Oh, Lord, you girls are not that important.* Somebody probably should have honked and said, "Y'all are not all that!"

LOVE YOUR CLOTHES

I was a small-town girl dreaming of the big time, so I studied stars for style and beauty inspiration. My eyebrows were brushed and bushy because I worshipped Brooke Shields. I was obsessed with Heather Locklear's bangs. I watched *Knots Landing, Dynasty,* and *Dallas* for fashion tips, but I really gravitated toward the latest MTV style. Think early Madonna with lace gloves, teased-up hair with a scarf tied in a big floppy bow like in *Desperately Seeking Susan,* a miniskirt with cropped leggings underneath, and a combat boot. I could totally pull it off, right? I really got into the groove.

Daddy took Beth and me shopping every weekend. Bless his

heart, he was so patient, holding our purses while we tried on outfit after outfit at Brooks and the Limited. I always felt like I had an eye for what was cute. Sometimes my aunt Lila took us to Nashville and bought us stuff at fancy boutiques, like Guess jeans with zippers at the ankles and Norma Kamali tops with huge shoulder pads. I just loved all that!

Beth's style was more formal than mine. She dressed up every day for school in pumps, a silk blouse, and designer jeans. On the way into school, we had to walk through the smoking porch past some rough girls. They threatened to beat me up once. Why do girls want to fight? I never had any interest in that. It is crazy to me! Beth, with her big purse and silk jumpsuit, spun around and got a mean, protective look on her face, gritted her teeth, pointed her finger at them, and said, "Don't. You. Dare. Bother. Her. I will ruin you." They never spoke to me again. She would fight a circle saw for me.

BEING FUN GETS YOU NOTICED

The school's music director, Mr. Bunch, a doll, insisted I join the school choir. It was a big deal to be in the choir because they traveled to perform at other schools and churches.

I said to him, "You know my voice is pitiful."

He said, "Yes, it is. But it doesn't matter. Just stand in the front, move your mouth, and dazzle, girl."

It's possible Mr. Bunch just wanted someone fun on the bus instead of another smart aleck or troublemaker. We did have a ball calling each other "darling" and laughing until we were weak. But the real reason he put me in front? I was window dressing. And let me tell you, I made that choir look good with my big hair and my glossed lips that moved in sync. The audience had no idea I didn't sing a note.

Senior year, the drama teacher asked me to play Stupefyin' Jones in a production of *Li'l Abner*. I'd never been in a high school musical before, but I was the only one who could pull off this particular role. *Li'l Abner* was set in a fictional town called Dogpatch, and Stupefyin' Jones was Dogpatch's version of a bombshell. My entire purpose was to gyrate around the stage— and I was thrilled to do it. My costume was a one-piece turquoise leotard with polka dots, a wide purple belt, and a low heel. Every other kid on the stage wore ripped Dogpatch-worthy jeans and T-shirts, while I sashayed around with big Barbie hair, popping my hip. I couldn't compare to Julie Newmar, who played the part in the movie, but my gyrations were pretty good, and the audience laughed. That high school musical was my first exposure to showbiz, and I felt like I was supposed to be there. It felt right. I was good at it. I know how to put on a show.

Afterward, I found my parents in the audience and was taken aback when Daddy said, "Why did you do that? You didn't even have one line!" I was hurt by that. To him, it was all about my reputation, and gyrating in a leotard wasn't how I safeguarded it. Looking back, I see he was just being a protective dad, and I understand why it bothered him.

When Mama saw how upset I was, she said, "Oh my gosh, you were so beautiful up there. You've got the cutest figure." I felt so much better after that.

YOU CAN'T MAJOR IN PRETTY

If you're told something your whole life—that being cute will make your life easier and get you a husband with a pension— you believe it. I genuinely believed that as long as I dazzled, I didn't have to worry about anything else. That turned out not to be true.

When Daddy started asking what I planned to do after high school, I had no idea. Beth went to Austin Peay State University in Clarksville, just twenty minutes from our house. In college, she broke fully out of her shyness shell, joined a sorority, was voted homecoming queen, and appeared in the Sigma Chi national calendar. She just bloomed. Daddy wanted to see me do as well as Beth and go to college.

Secretly, I thought, *I don't need college. I'm going to be a Hollywood star.* If I said that out loud, though, people would think I was a loon. On the other hand, it never dawned on me to drive to Los Angeles in my used Monte Carlo to find fortune and fame. I had big dreams, but I was so sheltered that I didn't know what to do with them. So I just avoided the whole discussion. I was cute and fun! My future was safe! Why even talk about it?

Halfway through my senior year, Daddy had had enough of my stalling. He sat me down and said, "Leanne, you can either join the military or go to college. You have to choose." Signing up for the military was definitely out. I was way too sissy for that. But college didn't feel right either.

Little Aunt Lila suggested I just get a job. "Leanne, you'd make a good secretary," she said. She didn't know I took typing in high school and hated it. All my friends could just type, type, type. They could pay attention, file, take notes, plan events. They had incredible skills in areas where I was hopeless. They were so good at organizing, they could have run the United States of America. A few of them got jobs as executive assistants in Nashville and are very successful. I was not cut out for that. I decided I'd go to college.

The night before I took the ACT at Austin Peay, I stayed up until 3:00 watching *The Benny Hill Show* in Beth's dorm room. Adams didn't have cable yet; Beth did, and I was fascinated. How did she get anything done?

The morning of the exam, I stopped at McDonald's on the way and burned my mouth on hot coffee. Exhausted, the roof of my mouth scalded, I was in no shape to take the test. I couldn't concentrate. One question involved figuring out how many times a hummingbird flapped its wings in a minute. It was simple math, and I knew I got that one right. I love a hummingbird. Overall, though, I was so intimidated.

When my scores came in, I showed them to Mr. Bunch. He said, "You can't get into Indiana School for the Blind with these!" And yet, somehow, the University of Tennessee in Knoxville accepted me. (The requirements in the '80s were a lot lower than they are now, praise the Lord.) My parents were relieved, and I was happy to make them happy.

WHAT DOES DAZZLING REALLY GET YOU?

Mama believed that Beth and I were born stunners. "Y'all are so beautiful," she told us daily. "Where in the world did y'all come from?" I thought she was building us up and appreciated her for it. Years later, I saw a guest on Oprah or Phil Donahue say that prioritizing pretty to your daughters, like my generation's parents did, was a bad idea because it would give them skewed values and self-hate, tying up their self-worth with their appearance. Oops! Too bad I saw that episode long after I'd already messed it up with my daughters.

There's a saying among my people: "All crows think theirs are the blackest." So when my girls, Maggie and Tess, were younger, I told them how pretty they were. I couldn't help it! I sounded just like Lucille, saying, "Y'all are so beautiful. Where did y'all come from?" (They are beautiful!)

But eventually, I also tried to break the generational message that being pretty is the key to a happy life. I tried to teach my children that self-worth can be found in their relationship with God. "It doesn't matter what you have, what you look like, or what you've done. You're a child of God. When you have self-doubt, focus on that," I told them. I really believe that, based on my own personal experience. The truth is, beauty fades. Money and status can be gone in a heartbeat. The things of this world are unsustainable. If all you care about is stuff, you're left with nothing when you lose it. And that is *so not pretty*. Or fun.

But if you have a deeper sense of purpose, superficial things like the size of your pores and some wrinkles by your eyes don't matter as much. Your purpose in life is not perfect contouring. It's helping people and, for me, hopefully giving them a little joy. You can lose money, a job, your house—and especially your teenage metabolism and collagen. But no one and nothing can take away your relationship with God.

In the end, being pretty got me only so far. If I'd focused on faith instead of counting on beauty as a saving grace, I might have been less scared about my future when I was just starting out.

In the pit of my stomach, I knew college wasn't going to work out well. I'd never been much of a student. I was too busy doing my hair.

As it turned out, you can't major in pretty in college.

So I majored in crazy boyfriends instead.

My Brief Life in Pageantry

I just got off a call with a TV showrunner from Louisville, Kentucky, a woman who is very successful in Hollywood and has nothing to prove to anyone. She said, "Everything's a pageant for us southern girls. I knew I was getting on this call with you and I had to zhuzh up my hair." Here's the thing: It was a voice-only call. That's just how deep the beauty obsession goes.

Nearly all southern girls have walked in at least one Little Miss or county fair pageant growing up. When Beth was eighteen, she was still an introvert, but she also knew she was tall, slim, and a looker. So she entered the Miss Tennessee pageant in Nashville, and I went with her to be her beauty helper. I thought I knew enough about doing hair and makeup, but I was way out of my league at Miss Tennessee. Beth and I walked into the backstage area with a makeup bag and a blowdryer. The other contestants came with an entourage of stage mothers, professional makeup artists, hairstylists, and smile consultants. The pageant people were hard-core. I overheard one contestant tell another, "Daddy flew me to the Bahamas last week to get a tan for this."

No one was going to fly us anywhere to get a tan, so we had to improvise. I put a darker shade of foundation on Beth's face, but that only made the rest of her seem paler. She wore a white bathing suit with black heels. It was a terrible decision. She looked like a ghost standing in a bucket. We were just two country girls who didn't know what we were doing. It's a testament to how stunning Beth was that she won "Most Photogenic" at that pageant.

When I was seventeen, I walked in my own pageant: the Robertson County Fairest of the Fair. The fair happened every summer and had games like darts and water guns, funnel cakes, and the 4-H baking competition. It was a big deal in our little world. We lived in the middle of nowhere and didn't have a lot going on. That once-a-year excitement meant something to me, and being in the pageant was the pinnacle of it.

For a week leading up to the pageant, I practiced walking in heels, checking myself in a mirror. I ate only one can of tuna a day. By the day of the fair, I was weak as water and couldn't even make a fist. My gosh, I was so thin. But everyone was thin back then. We didn't eat processed foods. I liked pinto beans more than white flour and sugar.

At the fair, the pageant contestants got to ride in a parade, so I sat up high on the back seat of a convertible, wearing a borrowed yellow dress and waving at the crowd. It was so humid you couldn't have fit my hair inside a bushel basket, but I was pretty cute.

The yellow dress was just a warm-up look. For the actual competition, my parents bought me a long white sequined gown with one arm off the shoulder. I walked well and was pretty enough to land in the top ten. As we came out for the semifinal, we were supposed to turn to the left in a complete circle for the judges. I knew what I was supposed to do, but for some crazy reason, I turned the opposite direction as everyone else. And those butthole judges cut me for making a bad pivot! I definitely would have been in the top five if I'd gone in the right direction.

I went backstage to kick myself over that, and a pageant mom approached me. I thought she'd say something sweet, like, *You did great, hon. Hold your head up high.* But she actually said, "You need to take six inches off your hair." When I looked at the pictures years later, I had to agree. My hair did look like it'd been chewed off by a dog.

My first thought after the loss: *Okay, I can do better. I'll figure out how the game works.*

My second thought: *This whole thing is just silly.*

I stand by that. I never walked in a pageant again.

CHAPTER 3

Attracted to Crazy

Your college years are supposed to be a time of discovery. You move away from the security and comfort of home, meet new people, try new things, act like an idiot, and make terrible decisions that hopefully you won't regret for the rest of your life.

Good times.

The persona I tried on for size in college? Well, I thought I was Erica Kane on *All My Children*. I was young and stupid and had Big Diva Dreams. Erica was always dramatic and had men chasing after her. I wanted men to fall at my feet too. I dreamed of breaking hearts and crying big, sloppy tears on the couch while wearing clip-on diamond earrings. And so my dating life was defined by high drama with pitiful boys. Some of them you wouldn't wipe your feet on.

MY FIRST LOVE

Back in high school, the hot spot for the teenagers of Robertson County wasn't the skating rink or the downtown one-screen movie theater. After we made loops around the local McDonald's, we'd park at the far end of the Kroger parking lot, hang out, lean on cars, and chat while adults went inside to buy milk. Some people slipped around and drank beer and smoked cigarettes. Not me. I was scared to death of alcohol. I don't like all that! I was very straightlaced. If any of my friends had two beers, I'd freak out and want to go home.

The first time I went there, I was fifteen. I had to beg Beth to take me with her to the world-famous Kroger parking lot. "Just don't embarrass me," she said.

As soon as we got there, a shirtless boy who weighed less than me—a tiny thing I could have held in my arms like a baby, but precious in jeans—walked over from across the parking lot. He had sweet eyes and feathered hair like David Cassidy. "Hey, you're Leanne Fletcher, right?" he said. "I've seen you around." He was standing pretty close. "Whoa, what is that *smell*?"

"It's meat and dog," I said. "You'll get used to it."

Let's say his name was William. He was two years older, a senior at Springfield High School, the big-city school in the county. I flipped my hair and batted my mascara-covered eyelashes at him. When Beth saw me flirting, she made a beeline for William and said, "Don't you dare talk to her!" She would have reacted that way to my flirting with anyone; she thought I was too young to even be there, much less talk to a boy.

Beth looked like she wanted to whip that sweet kid. My sister was protective and bossy, more like a mother than a sister to me. She was the one to tell me to "stand up straight" and "pull up your socks." Lucille was more like an encouraging best friend.

Beth pulled me away from William and said, "Watch your reputation, Leanne," in the same tone Daddy would've said it. They were both obsessed with watching our reputations, like someone was going to come along and steal them at any second. I didn't want to ruin my reputation, but I also thought, *Who cares?* How was talking to a darling boy in the parking lot going to ruin my reputation? I wasn't smoking crack behind a dumpster. She was acting like the mother of us all, like Martha Washington. Lord!

Beth could be very intimidating when she was mad. William valued his life, so he didn't try to talk to me again that night. When we got home, Beth whispered to Mom so Dad couldn't hear, "Leanne flirted with a boy in the parking lot." Lucille just gave me an "It's all right, baby" look. She never made me feel ashamed or belittled. She later told me, "God doesn't hold you accountable for anything you do until the age of twenty-one anyway." I don't think that's biblical. (I was raised Methodist. I learned forgiveness and love, but I don't know Scripture.) Mama didn't say a word to Beth. My sister ratted me out and then went straight to her room to cut out pictures of Lee Majors and Farrah Fawcett from *Teen Beat* to put in her albums, slamming the door on her way in.

The next day, William called the house and asked me on a date. I said yes in half a heartbeat. I was dying to ride around in his '79 Monte Carlo that was as big as a yacht. "You can go on a date with him," warned Beth, "but so help me, you better sit on the far side of that bench seat. Don't you dare sit next to him in the middle." She scared the life out of me. When the time came, I sat as far away from William as possible.

We drove to the mall to walk around and had dinner at Mr. Gatti's Pizza, famous for its buffet. You could get slices of every topping known to man and take them to a plastic table that was bolted to the floor. I didn't want to eat much in front of William, so I took only one bite of my meat supreme slice. He told me about his family. They were tobacco farmers like my family on both sides. His mom was a teacher, and I liked that his people were kind of hoop-dee-doo. People saw us sitting together and said hello. Everyone knew and loved William, and I could see why. He was so sweet and fun, just a nice guy. When he dropped me off at home, I thought, *Well, I guess this means I'm going to marry him.*

We stayed together that whole year and spent every spare minute together, driving around, parking in his family's tobacco fields, necking. William spent so much time at my house that he would fall asleep on my couch watching TV with his head on my shoulder. When I was a junior, he left for the University of Tennessee, and our relationship was on-and-off for a couple of years. We both kissed other people during the "off" periods, but I still believed he was going to be my husband. I applied to UT in the first place because William was there. If we were living on the same campus, we'd be back "on." Then he'd get his degree and we'd get married. It was a given.

In the meantime, I had to stick it out at UT, a place that overwhelmed me. Until then, I had no idea how sheltered I'd been. Adams had only five hundred people, and my graduation class was just forty-two kids. Knoxville was a massive city of two hundred thousand, and the student body of UT consisted of thirty-three thousand. The football stadium sat one hundred thousand people! The sheer quantity of faces—many of which didn't look like me or anyone in my hometown—that went by me every day boggled my brain. On the plus side, I could get pizza delivered to my dorm room.

The first few weeks, I clung to William like a life preserver. I ate with him in the cafeteria, followed him around campus, pestered him about when he was getting out of class so we could meet up. I insisted on going with him to football games and frat parties and draped myself on him like a second jacket. I called him three, four, five times a day. I might, just might, have come off as a bit needy. I probably worried that little thing to death.

William was an overachiever in class and a cadet in the ROTC. But he was into his fraternity, and during downtime, he always wanted to hang out with his brothers. I made the effort to fit into his new life, which meant going to parties with tons of trashed, sweaty people. At one party, William wandered off and left me alone with a bunch of men chanting "chug" at one another like savages. I found him on the dance floor, singing along to "Super Freak" by Rick James at the top of his lungs, a Solo cup of beer in one hand and a cigarette in the other. Pretty tame stuff in hindsight, but I was just coming off the United Methodist Youth Fellowship. I thought partying was wrong. *I shouldn't be here*, I thought. *This is gross. And my shoes are sticking to the floor.*

I pulled William to the side and said, "What are you doing? What are *we* doing?" I believed we were really and truly bound for marriage, and I didn't like it that my future husband was partying so much. "I want you to stop drinking and smoking and spend more time with me," I declared. Admittedly, I cramped his style and smothered him, but I was only trying to help *him*!

Three weeks into my freshman year, after another Sodom and Gomorrah Saturday night, I started nagging William again the next day. He held up his hand to stop me from talking and said, "Leanne, you're not fun."

What in the world? Not fun? I was *so fun*! "Here lies Leanne Morgan. She was fun" is going to be written on my tombstone. If he'd said, "And you're not cute either," I might've broken into a million pieces.

"I can't take your nagging and clinging anymore," he said. "I think we should break up."

I was crushed. We'd broken up before, but this time felt final. I mourned for each one of the six babies I would never have with William. I'd never felt more lost. I'd come to Knoxville for him, for us. Without him, I couldn't think of a single reason to stay. For months after the breakup, I grieved. My relationship, over. My vision for the future, destroyed. When I found the motivation to go to class, I struggled academically and failed tests.

My little daddy cried with me on the phone when he learned William had dumped me. "Are you okay?" he asked.

I lied to protect his feelings. "I'm fine. Are y'all okay?"

"We're fine. Do you need anything?"

"No, thanks. I'm fine."

Mom got on the phone and said, "Everything's going to be all right."

"I'm going to flunk out," I said. "I don't know what I'm doing."

"When are you supposed to start your period?" she asked.

I slammed the phone down, hanging up on her, and then called right back. "I'm sorry," I said. "My period's coming tomorrow."

"You're going to be okay," she promised.

I prayed she was right.

For the rest of my freshman fall semester, I hid in my dorm room, watched daytime soaps on a tiny TV set, and cried over Purina dog food commercials. Oh, the misery! Erica Kane and her heartache had nothing on me.

THE REBOUND

It was hard for me to be alone. (I hate that about my younger self.) If I didn't have a boyfriend, I at least needed to have a crush, a cute boy to keep my eye on. I had to have something going on to distract me from the fact that I was flunking out.

William was too normal for me, I decided. Too well-adjusted. I wanted to date boys who were completely wrong for me. Ideally, they'd be twisted, be damaged, make terrible decisions, and, I don't know, hate their mamas. Stability? Kindness? Blech . . . A relationship had to be high drama to be interesting. That said, I didn't want to date a partier. Drunk and stupid held no appeal. I wanted a brooder, someone deep and messed up who needed a good girl—like me—to fix him.

It's not like I invented being a drama queen with a thirst for twisted boys. Other girls in my dorm grew up sheltered too and came to college to act like idiots. We dated stupid boys and cried rivers of tears after they dumped us. We just *ate it,* over and over again. And somehow, the drama of getting our hearts handed to us was the only thing we cared about.

I met one boy at a frat party while visiting Beth at Austin Peay for a weekend. I spotted him on the dance floor. He was real cute. He had rhythm. I moonwalked over to him and introduced myself.

We'll call him Mark. He was a sophomore, and he played on the baseball team. His mama was from central Tennessee. His father was a professor whose people came from Puerto Rico. I was always attracted to people of different ethnicities. When I was growing up, everyone I knew was white, except for my grandmama Emma's second husband, my step-granddaddy, Frank, who was half Mexican and half Arapaho. Frank had a little round tummy, beautiful dark skin, and tattoos of stars on his hands that fascinated me. Once a paratrooper in the U.S. Army, he danced with my little grandmama around the kitchen and spoke so sweetly in Spanish to her. I thought he was the kindest, most attentive husband I'd ever seen, and I worshipped him. If I could be wooed by someone like Frank, I'd be in heaven.

Mark didn't know Spanish, sadly, but he was athletic and could dance like Michael Jackson, which set me on fire. That seemed like reason enough to date him.

One night on a walk, we started talking about our dreams for the future. He said, "I want to play in a summer softball league and get a government job. I probably won't make much money, but I don't care. I would be happy with $30,000 a year for the rest of my life."

Okay, that wasn't crazy, as in dramatic. That was just plain nuts.

I said, "Mark, honey, this isn't going to work out." For someone to decide at twenty that he didn't care about financial security gave me the ick. I wasn't a gold digger. But there was no point in dating a man who wanted his wife to be the breadwinner. I wanted a brooder *with potential*! Someone who was twisted now but who would make a good living once I straightened him out.

He was surprised to hear it. "What? Why?"

How to explain? "Well, I'm attracted to crazy in the short term. But, long term, I'm very attracted to ambition. I'm going to need a man in a button-down and khaki pants who's good at math and has a 401(k)."

He was offended that I called him crazy. Fair. He grieved harder for me than our relationship warranted, calling me three, four, five times a day and asking, "Can we meet and talk this through one more time?" (Now I knew how William felt.) I blew him off—what young people now call "ghosting"—and that messed with his head. I wasn't trying to make him suffer. It just happened. When I wasn't getting dumped, I was a real heartbreaker.

THE NICE GUY

The guy I'll call Brendan was a super smart aeronautic engineering major at UT. He looked like a cartoon pilot, with a square jaw, beefy forearms, and slicked-back black hair. He became an actual pilot for American Airlines later in life.

He wooed me hard, taking me to nice restaurants and paying for everything. He was sweet, kind, courteous . . . and he bored me to death. Dates with him were hard for me to get through. Brendan wasn't brooding and dramatic, so I wasn't interested. Yet I kept going out with him anyway.

One night, the plan was to have dinner at a Mexican restaurant and then see *Rhinestone,* starring Dolly Parton and Sylvester Stallone. I loved them both and was excited to see this movie. But first I had to endure a whole meal with Brendan.

He ordered us a pitcher of sangria to go with our meal. I had no idea what sangria was, but it was sweet and yummy and went down easy. Before we even got our food, I was looped. I had zero experience being drunk, and I stumbled out of that restaurant in my pumps with a belly full of chimichangas. While we drove to the theater, I started feeling sentimental and rambled on about my dog back home and how I kissed him on the mouth. Brendan looked at me with an "ewww" expression. We hadn't kissed yet. *She hasn't kissed me but she kisses dogs?* Or maybe he just thought, *She's a nutjob.*

As soon as I sat down in the theater, my seat started spinning. I planted my feet on the floor to try to make it stop. The chimichangas were a-stirring. I had never been that kind of sick in my life, but I didn't want to miss the Dolly movie. Sylvester was so tiny! He looked like he was five foot two in a little bitty rhinestone jumpsuit. You could see the outline of his do-ings!

By some miracle, I didn't vomit during the movie, but I came close. I told Brendan he had to drive me home before things got real bad. He grimaced but said, "Okay." When we got back to campus, Brendan sweetly helped me into my room and steered me so I fell on my bed and not the floor. Once he was sure I was lying on my side (in case I puked), he sat with me for a minute until I told him I wanted to be alone. "I understand," he said. "Call me if you need anything." And he took off. He was so gentlemanly. It *really* got on my nerves.

It was a few days before the start of the summer semester, and most of the students hadn't moved into their dorms yet. About ten minutes after Brendan left, I staggered toward the communal bathroom at the end of the hall, fell to my hands and knees, and lost my dinner on the floor every few feet as I crawled the rest of the way. I had my head in the toilet all night. I thought I was going to die, and there was no one around to help me. I probably had alcohol poisoning. I have not had a sip of sangria since.

The next day, I woke up in my unmade bed, still dressed, with dried puke on my shirt. I was disgusted with myself and assumed I'd never hear from Brendan again.

But that sweet fool kept calling me.

The really twisted part of my relationship with Brendan was that he was kind, had ambition, took me to nice places, and was always such a gentleman, but he made me sick. I didn't know what I wanted. I was so broken, God help me, and I took it out on these poor boys. If I could go back and talk to myself as that college student, I'd say, *Oh, my darling, it's okay that you vomited. I know you're embarrassed. Everything's going to work out.*

THE VERY BAD DECISION

By my sophomore year, I was supposed to choose a major, and I was no closer to figuring that out than I'd been my first week on campus. I felt an ache, a longing, for something or someone to just tell me what to do with my life.

While I was filling up William's car at a gas station (we'd stayed friends; I can't remember why I had his car that day), a super handsome guy pulled up next to me at the pump and started talking to me. I'll call him Evan. He was older than me—by six years, I later learned—and said he was on campus to play intramural sports with his old fraternity. That seemed stupid, but he was stunning, so I let it go.

As we were chatting, he paused and just stared at me for a beat. Then he said, "You're the most beautiful girl I've ever seen." My low self-esteem was blown away by that. We talked at the gas pump for hours. Cars drove up and honked at us to move, and we talked on. He wooed me, and I was so flattered by it. I saw myself as a country bumpkin, and he was this sophisticated guy from Connecticut. And did I say *stunning*? One of his jobs was being a fit model for the company that makes uniforms for the NFL. He had the body of a wide receiver: big booty, bulging thighs and calves, tiny waist, and sleek but toned upper body. I swooned.

During our early dates, we just hung out together, taking long walks and talking. He didn't shower me with flowers and fancy restaurant meals like Brendan, which I found honest and authentic. I'd never laughed so much with a man as I did with Evan. We were just tickled with each other, and our relationship felt natural and healthy.

But Evan wasn't so healthy himself. He was tormented by a mysterious sadness. I'd catch him sitting quietly and looking gloomy for no apparent reason. He was insecure about his looks too. He'd ask me, "Are you staring at my hair? It looks so bad. You can tell me." He talked constantly about how bad his skin was and whether he was balding, and he obsessed about the fact that he wasn't in as good shape as he used to be. I'd asked for brooding and dramatic, but this was exhausting. He was as insecure about his looks as a woman. I'd taken a couple of psychology classes by then, and I recognized a damaged soul. I thought, *Evan is in pain. He needs me. I think I can fix him.*

How naïve of me.

He wanted to fix me too. I told him how confused and directionless I felt about school and life. I'd been thinking about dropping out for a while but hadn't told my parents or Beth because I knew they'd worry about me. Evan said, "If you aren't getting anything out of college, you should drop out and do something that's right for you." He had no idea what that might be, and neither did I. I loved doing makeup. Maybe I'd make a living out of that? I read the Help Wanted section in the newspaper and saw an ad for a job at the Clinique counter at a nearby mall. He encouraged me to apply for it.

Right now, you are probably thinking, *Leanne, don't quit college! Stick with it! You're halfway there. Get that degree, honey!*

I was an idiot. I dropped out and took the mall job. And the bad decisions kept coming.

For starters, I moved in with Evan after a month of dating. I wasn't raised that way, and I knew it was wrong. I was lost in so many ways. If you want the relationship to last, shacking up is a bad move. And yet we had fun at that little apartment. When it was good, our relationship was wonderful. But when it was bad, it was very dysfunctional. Our relationship was like swinging between two extremes. There was no middle ground with Evan. I clung to the belief that his good side was so great it compensated for his dark side.

Fun Evan told me repeatedly how beautiful I was. We called each other "baby" and "precious" and snuggled under a blanket on the couch to watch old movies. We had the same sense of humor and the same taste in music, and we talked nonstop about everything. He was so tickled by my jokes and belly-laughed at each one.

Bad Evan was insecure and super critical. For long periods, he wouldn't speak to me. He locked me out of the apartment. If he thought a man was looking at me, he'd take a swing at him. We were thrown out of concerts and parties because of his jealous temper.

I justified all that in my head because he was passionate and his emotions were so deep. And, as I said, the good times were really good. When Evan proposed spontaneously, I was flooded with relief. Being engaged made it okay that we'd been living together. I had a feeling getting married was a mistake, but I couldn't stop it. I felt like I was stuck on this runaway train and couldn't jump off.

We shared the news over dinner with his parents, hoop-dee-doo people from up north who'd moved to Chattanooga. I made the toast: "To getting married and having a bunch of babies!" I was taken aback when Evan's parents didn't clink glasses. His mother said, "You don't need children right away." His father nodded vigorously. *What in the world?* They'd just shot down their own future grandbabies. Who were these people? I had a sinking spell right there at the table.

My parents didn't approve of the relationship either. It shames me to say that Evan acted like Lucille and Jimmy, sweet country people, were beneath him. He talked down to them. He did the same to me, but I didn't have the best self-esteem at twenty, and I just accepted it.

We had a traditional church wedding in Adams with nuts,

mints, and a cake in the fellowship hall. Evan didn't have many guests there because they were from up north, but they sent nice gifts. The people from Adams gave us things to set up housekeeping, like towels, dishes, and sheets. A little woman with dementia gave us a fake floral arrangement that played the theme from *Star Wars* when you turned it on. It's my favorite floral arrangement to this day.

It will not surprise anyone to learn that Evan and I were not happy newlyweds. Get a load of this: A few weeks into our marriage, he told me I needed diction lessons. My accent was too country, according to him, and people were saying I was stupid behind my back. When he said all this to me, I nodded, but even with my low self-esteem, I never believed he was right. I thought, *You're not going to change me.* I'm glad I didn't listen to him! Being myself is what made things happen for me in my career later on. This is who I am. You either like it or you don't. And it's okay if you don't! (But I hope you do.)

Once, my parents sent me some new clothes as a gift. Evan was so jealous of my close relationship with them that he threw all the clothes out the window into a tree. He stopped letting Lucille and Jim visit me. He wouldn't open the door for my friends. He had isolated me from everyone I cared about. He couldn't hold a job and bounced from one to another. I walked on eggshells because of his volatility. I never knew when he'd explode.

Meanwhile, I worked three jobs to support us. One was answering the phone and sweeping up hair at a salon; another was at a clothing store. The best one was doing makeup consults at Miller's department store. I had a ball at that job. As soon as I touched a woman's face, she would open up and tell me all her problems. It was like Mama in the office at Fletcher's Meat Processing. I tried to make the women laugh and gave them advice if they asked for it. I was like a therapist. Helping them made me feel better about the bad marriage I was stuck in.

What gave me hope during that bleak time was thinking, *This isn't it for me. One day, I'm going to Hollywood.* I never stopped believing I was going to get a job in showbiz in the future. I didn't know how or what, but I was going to do it. At my lowest point, my dreams pulled me up. *My life might be horrible now, but something's coming,* I told myself. *Something great.*

Two years went by, and Evan just got meaner, more jealous, and more physical with me. The last straw came at Christmastime. Evan and I went to a restaurant before going shopping. We sat down and ordered ice teas. He got mad over something—I can't remember what—and pitched a fit before storming off and leaving me with no ride and no cash.

I had to tell the waitress, a downtrodden older woman, "I don't have any money to pay for our drinks."

She gave me a knowing look and said, "Honey, it's all right. Don't worry about it."

This was what I call "a God moment." I could just tell from the look in her eyes that she'd been through something bad herself. Her compassion and words of comfort brought me to a decision. God said to me, *This woman is your sign.* In my mind's eye, I could see God shutting a door on that marriage.

After all those terrible decisions, I made a great one. I divorced Evan, and let me tell you, it was such a relief! Like losing 190 unwanted pounds. I never looked back.

I thought I was attracted to crazy, but I got a lot more than I bargained for with Evan. My first marriage might have fulfilled my Erica Kane drama dreams, but when the dust settled after my divorce at twenty-three, having a "boring" relationship started to look pretty good.

CHAPTER 4

As Broke as a Church Mouse

Where I was raised, everyone had roughly the same standard of living. Houses were the same size. No one had mansions. We had the same cars. And it was enough. We were all fine. No one was dirt-poor. No one was starving. Everyone owned land (that was worth a lot!) and their homes. I thought we were all well-off. And if some people in Adams did have more, they didn't show it because that wouldn't have been polite.

It wasn't until I went to college that I came face-to-face with wealthy people. On day one, I met a bunch of rich private-school girls from Chattanooga and Memphis. As soon as I opened my mouth, they said, "Listen to her accent!" I was probably the first country bumpkin they'd ever seen up close.

I thought I was the height of sophistication in my oversize white painter's overalls and orange crop top. My hair was all teased up with a floppy bow, like the band Bananarama. These girls looked to me like they'd just walked off the pages of *The Official Preppy Handbook* or modeled for Pappagallo. Their hair was stick straight, which was an incredible accomplishment in the days before antifrizz serum. They wore kelly-green and shell-pink Fair Isle sweaters and grosgrain belts with gold buckles in the shape of frogs.

I said to one of them, "That buckle is *so precious*! But why frogs?"

No one knew, or they just didn't want to tell me. Maybe frogs were a secret code the rich used to signal one another.

On move-in day, I noticed their cars were fancier than mine. I drove a used Monte Carlo that my aunt Lila and uncle Raymond bought for me. It had a T-top that I thought was so cute. These girls drove German cars I'd never heard of before. "What's a bee em double you?" I asked, which made them howl. At least they thought I was funny.

They said things like, "My family summers in Montana." "Summer" was a verb for these people. The farthest I'd traveled from home in my entire life was Panama City, Florida, for a family vacation. I'd also been to Gatlinburg and to 4-H camp in Columbia, Tennessee. Columbia just so happens to be the mule capital of the world. Every year since 1840, they've celebrated Mule Day, an event that attracts two hundred thousand breeders and fans from all over. None of those rich girls had ever been to Mule Day, so I had that on them.

While I was growing up, my family never talked about what things cost or how much we earned. But rich people, I learned, *loved* to talk about money. "Where does your family money come from?" asked Melody, a girl from Chattanooga, five minutes after we met. "Is it old money or new money?" What in the world did that mean? Was I supposed to check the year on the five-dollar bill in my pocket?

My roommate, Lara, explained it to me. She said old money meant your family had been wealthy since your great-great-grandparents' time. Old money was snobby and kind of quiet. Everyone knew you had it, so you didn't have to show it off. You wore pricey but boring clothes, lived in old mansions with leaky roofs, and drove old German cars. New money meant your daddy or granddaddy got rich, and you had to advertise the wealth to everyone to prove how special and important you were. You wore flashy designer clothes, lived in enormous McMansions, and drove brand-new German cars.

I didn't have any idea what she was talking about. I just rolled my eyes.

All along, I thought my family was well-off because we had land, owned our business, shopped at the Limited in Nashville, and had a car *and* a truck. The Fletchers were never any kind of rich. But we had our very own Coca-Cola machine, so take that, Melody!

For the most part, the rich girls treated me well, like their poor country mascot. They tried to outdo one another with their possessions, but I wasn't a threat since I didn't have any of that stuff. I didn't compete with them over the size of their tennis bracelets. I didn't know what a tennis bracelet was. We didn't have a tennis court where I grew up, much less a diamond bracelet to wear when playing.

Sometimes, though, they could be mean as snakes. One night, Harriet, a girl in my dorm, said to me with complete honesty, "I want people to wilt in my presence." I thought, *What does that even mean?* It was just so bizarre. She needed to feel superior to other people because being rich wasn't enough. Then again, her mama was downright cruel to her, telling her she never measured up. That woman was a butthole, and it made Harriet a bit of one too.

Lara's grandparents owned a funeral home in Knoxville, and we went to their house for dinner sometimes. All their stuff was gorgeous: gold fixtures, crystal glasses, furniture upholstered in beautiful fabrics. I'd never seen anything like it. Her grand-mother was out of town one night, and she told Lara we could get a bag of shrimp out of the freezer. Lara opened their deep freeze and, I kid you not, it was full of frozen shrimp.

Who were these people? Where I grew up, shrimp was a vacation food. This family had fifty pounds of it in the deep freeze, ready to be cooked on a whim. Who were they, the Ken-nedys?

All the girls in the dorm rushed sororities, so I did too. The Chi Omega girls reminded me of young Barbara Bush. They were old money, conservative, and, Lord, they had terrible bobs. Some looked like Dana Carvey as the Church Lady on *Satur-day Night Live*. I really didn't fit in, but I wanted to join because Beth was a Chi O at Austin Peay, and she said I was a sure thing because I was a legacy. They cut me anyway. (Fun fact: My daughter Maggie was a Chi O at UT. They've changed a lot since my day.)

As soon as I walked into Phi Mu, the next place I rushed, I thought, *Lord, these are the most stunning people I've ever seen.* The new-money girls of Phi Mu were jazzy, like those sorority recruitment videos on YouTube, with fifty Blake Lively blondes in matching bikinis and Greek letters on their boobs. Glamor-ous and willowy, they moved like beauty queens and talked like movie stars. Some were cheerleaders (a very big deal at UT), and one had been Miss Tennessee.

Phi Mu chose me. Part of me was flattered. Part of me wor-ried about the extra expense. I hated the idea of asking my mom and dad to pay the dues. And what was the point of joining if I was going to marry William soon and leave college? I was such a ding-dong.

For a week, I went through the motions. But with every day

that passed, I realized more that I didn't give a crap. I couldn't make myself care about any of it. So I dropped out. When the chapter president, a sweet girl with teeth so bright I had to shield my eyes, asked why I wanted to quit, I said, "I need to focus on my studies."

Maybe I would have stayed if they served shrimp. Hard to say.

TRASH TALK

The gulf between old money and new money didn't seem all that big to me. But the gap between urban and rural was as wide as the Grand Canyon. It was like we didn't even speak the same language.

I showed an English paper to a girl from Memphis. She read it, handed it back, and said, "How are you even here?"

Some of my professors mocked me too. One English teacher, a little old woman from up north, marked my papers with big red circles and wrote comments like "This is not part of the English language" and "Your grammar is atrocious."

I came from a pocket in rural Tennessee where people speak with a dialect that has unique phrasing and pronunciations, a mishmash of Irish, Welsh, and other immigrant languages. For example, I grew up using the word "saunder," as in, "She saundered across the room." Apparently, the correct word is "saunter." Who knew?

If I happened to pronounce a word wrong (like "epitome" or "Worcestershire"), the Chattanooga girls would roll on the floor laughing. If I wore "mall clothes," which I loved, they smirked at me. And the next thing I knew, I'd see them *saundering* around campus in the Guess jeans they stole right out of my closet.

Even though I had no idea what a BMW was, the private-school girls were up my butt to be my friend. I think they were drawn to me because I was authentic. Lord, I had flaws, terrible ones. I had no direction and low self-esteem. But unlike them, I didn't try to hide my crazy behind diamond tennis bracelets and velvet headbands. I put it right out there for the whole world to see.

FLAT BROKE AND HAVING A BALL

I've never been more broke in my life than after Evan and I split up. I was twenty-three, a college dropout, and a divorcée (but still cute and fun). I was down to one job by then, the makeup counter at Miller's, and I slept on my friend Alison's couch.

One day, Stan, who worked in security at Miller's, found me at the Clinique counter, like always. He and his buddy Brian from the shoe department—both students at UT—always came by to talk to me.

"Brian and I are renting an apartment together," he said. "It's in Fort Sanders. I know you're looking for a place to live. You could move in with us. The apartment has two floors. Brian and I will sleep on the bottom floor, and you can have the nice bedroom upstairs. We'll share the kitchen." With two roommates, I could afford to get off Alison's couch. I took a leap of faith to live with those two boys. It was definitely a God thing, not just for me, but for them too.

I've always enjoyed tending to people. I like to cook and wash clothes for them. Nothing made me happier than making a crockpot queso dip, heating up some tortilla chips, and serving it to Stan and Brian, full dazzle. I got all up in their personal business like a mother hen every time they left the house. Whenever they went out, I'd say, "Be careful, y'all!"

Self-sufficient Stan didn't need much help. Darling Brian, on the other hand, was a *disaster*. He had the maturity level of a toddler, was chronically late, and barely passed his classes. Naturally, I doted on him like an overly involved big sister.

I was still healing from my divorce and felt like an outcast. I had no money to spend, so I stayed in my little bedroom, listening to the Cure and Patsy Cline, crying and grieving on Saturday nights. Brian and Stan went to frat parties. And Brian sometimes brought girls home. On Sunday mornings, these sweet coeds would leave our apartment through the kitchen while I sat at the table drinking coffee and smoking a cigarette in my ratty old robe.

With mascara running down their cheeks, they'd smile at me and say sheepishly, "Good morning." I'd smile back and think, *Honey, you just slept with a boy who writes bad checks.* It was wrong of me to judge them. Lord, I had no reason to judge anybody. I couldn't blame them for hooking up with Brian. They were as attracted to crazy as I used to be.

Stan and Brian had a darling group of friends who came over all the time. I'd make a big pan of nachos and feed them. They called me Lou. I was flattered by the attention. It was innocent and nurturing, like I was a house mama to these boys.

Once, Brian took his frat brothers on a tour though my panty drawer. When I found out, I could have died from embarrassment. He thought it was nifty that he was living with a young divorcée, and he just couldn't help showing off. I gave him a pass. I was grateful he didn't steal my panties and sell them.

Despite having a ball with these boys and loving my job at Miller's, I still worried I wasn't getting anywhere in life. Doing makeup consultations and sharing a dingy apartment couldn't be it for me. I was grasping for direction, looking for any sign to point me where I needed to go.

Around then, my supervisor asked whether I was interested in managing a new line of cosmetics. "It's a promotion with more money," she said, dangling a golden carrot in front of my face.

I barely got paid anything, so I thought, *This could be fabulous.* "Of course I'm interested," I said.

She wrote my new base salary on a piece of paper and slid it across the table to me. "You're going to be very happy with this," she said.

My heart nearly beat out of my body as I reached for the paper. I was so excited to see how much I was going to be making. Maybe enough to buy one of those bags of frozen shrimp or a frog belt buckle. I picked up the paper and looked at the number.

What in the world? It was pitiful, before poverty level. I couldn't live on that.

Holding that slip of paper, I had an epiphany: *I don't want to live like this.*

If I took that job, my life wouldn't go anywhere. In five years, I'd still be standing on my feet for eight hours in a little department store. My world would shrink to five square feet—the amount of space behind that counter. I knew in my heart I'd never be happy that way. The boys and I were having a ball being broke together, but they were going to finish their degrees soon. And then what would happen to me?

That piece of paper convinced me it was time to go back to school and get an education.

SOME MONEY IS BETTER THAN NONE

I knew going back to school was the right thing to do, but I had mixed feelings about it.

I said to Daddy, "I'm twenty-four, and everyone is going to be younger than me. I'll be twenty-six when I graduate. That is so old." Twenty-six was ancient to me then. In my young mind, two years felt like fifty.

"You're going to be twenty-six anyway," he replied. "Good night, you might as well get educated."

I thought, *My sweet daddy.* When he said that to me, it gave me hope. I got the little lift I needed.

My parents' love, patience, and faith in me was like a bottomless well that they drew from over and over. A lot of parents might not put their child through school after she'd dropped out. But my precious little daddy offered to pay my tuition, which I never would have been able to afford on my own.

I decided to major in child and family studies, with a focus on crisis intervention and counseling. I loved learning about people. I'd been in therapy and thought I could help other people who'd been through something by counseling them. It felt like a good fit for me. And I was sure I could earn a decent living doing that. But always in the back of my mind, I thought, *I could be a therapist, but I've also got that Hollywood thing going.*

I also did something truly radical, for me anyway. I went to a salon and got my hair chopped off. I'd always had long blond hair, but I had this overwhelming desire to get rid of everything and start over.

And I might save on shampoo and conditioner.

When I walked into the kitchen with my new look, Stan and Brian did a triple take. "Lou, what in the world?" asked Stan.

With my new look, I went out to find a better job. My parents were paying for my tuition, but I was still responsible for rent, food, and extras. Since I was taking classes during the day, I couldn't work at Miller's anymore, so I started waiting tables at Applebee's (just like my friend Nate Bargatze!). Before long, I moved on to Grady's, a local bar and grill known by UT students as the best restaurant job in Knoxville. A lot of students made so much money in tips that they dropped out of college. I was doing the reverse: First I dropped out, and then I served at Grady's.

One of my new coworkers said, "You look like Susan Powter with that hair." Powter was a fitness guru from the '80s, with buzzed platinum blond hair and the catchphrase "Stop the insanity!" That was not the look I was going for!

The servers at Grady's were a typical restaurant wild bunch. If you've ever worked in food service, you know what I'm talking about. They liked to have a good time. Not *all* of them were big drinkers. Some of them had a lot of sense. But not many of them went to church; I was sure about that.

I'm not a drinker and I've never done drugs, but I was smoking more than ever, puffing through a pack of cigarettes a day. I used to take a cigarette break with the line cooks by the dumpsters and listen to all their stories about jail. Not that they'd done hard time. They just got drunk and slept it off in a cell.

I had a ball with those guys. I loved everyone I worked with. The back lot was the place to be to find out who was dating who—a list that changed every week. But I stayed out of that mess. I'd had enough of dating. My schedule was already full to bursting with classes, homework, working five nights a week, and making sure Brian didn't hock my furniture.

From now on, I was going to hold my Susan Powter head high, make some money, get my degree, and figure out my future without some pitiful man turning my life upside down.

How to Flirt

I could go out and get a man tonight if I had to. He might not be a stable, successful man with all his teeth. But I could do it.

So could Lucille. She had a stroke and is in a wheelchair, but she could go out there and find a man tonight too. We know how to cut our eyes at a man to get his attention. But that's not what does it.

Flirting doesn't really have all that much to do with how you look or what you say. It's about how you make a man feel about himself.

Men need to be needed. They need to be useful. It's in their DNA to want to protect a woman. I tell the security team at every theater and arena I perform in, "Oh my gosh, I'm so thankful to y'all for keeping me safe!" I really mean that. And when these men (any man) hear that kind of "you're my hero" stuff, that you know they could kick in a door to save the day, they puff up their chests. In the right circumstances, they might even fall in love with you.

I love men. I need them. But in our society, the dynamic between men and women is changing fast. Women can take care of themselves. We are women, hear us roar! One young woman I work with wants a man so bad, and she's trying to date. But it never works out. She thinks men are intimidated by how successful she is. But I think she's so brilliant and competent that men feel they have nothing to offer her.

It's wonderful that men don't have to be the primary breadwinners anymore. But they still need to feel like they're protectors and providers. So if you want a man, you have to give him a chance to say, "I got this."

CHAPTER 5

Chase, Catch, Kill: Courtship in Your Twenties

In their dating years, some of my friends swore by the art of playing hard to get. "Men love a challenge," they said. "They get all riled up from the chase."

That may be. William chased me around the Kroger's parking lot in high school, but once he caught me and I got super clingy, he couldn't get rid of me fast enough. Evan wooed me hard, and I moved in with him way too fast. That one didn't end well either.

So there might be something to the idea that if a woman is too easy to catch, a man will lose interest in her. This dynamic is twisted and probably sexist, and it makes me afraid for my bighearted daughters. But there's no denying the kernel of truth in it.

In my post-divorce single life, with my "stop the insanity" short hair, I wasn't going to play hard to get, easy to get, or any other dating game. Patrick Swayze, who I loved, could have dirty-danced right into Grady's and tried to sweep me off my feet. He had a tiny fanny and great rhythm, but I would not have cha-chaed with him for a minute. I was rebuilding my life, and men were a distraction.

THE CHASE

During one shift at Grady's, I was standing against the brick wall between some ferns, talking with the other servers and waiting for our tables to get seated. A manager led a bunch of trainees though the restaurant. One of the trainees was six foot four, had clear blue eyes and broad shoulders, and was lean like Chuck Connors in *The Rifleman*.

As he passed by me, I said, "You're tall as a tree." Just a welcome, a hello. I didn't mean anything bad by it.

He looked at me and said "Sorry" like he was offended.

I thought, *Great, another butthole is coming to work at Grady's.* A lot of the staff had an attitude because we worked at the best place in town. I guessed this guy felt that way, so I made a mental note to avoid him.

The next day, Rifleman stood right next to me at the brick wall. I was talking my head off with my friends, and he didn't say a word. *He might be shy,* I thought. *Maybe not a butthole?*

A week later, the whole staff gathered for a shift meeting before the dinner service. The same guy sat right next to me in a booth. I was eating a big old baked potato, loaded with butter, sour cream, cheese, bacon, and chives. I was so tickled about it. He was eating cottage cheese on his baked potato. No wonder he was so skinny.

He leaned toward me and said, "You really don't need to eat all that fat."

What in the world?

Not shy, I thought. *Definitely a butthole.* Who tells a stranger she's eating too much fat? It was just so rude, I was speechless, but only for a second. I said, "I'm going to eat this potato, and I may eat another one."

If that was the last thing I ever said to him, it would be enough. What I didn't know yet was that this ding-dong had already fallen in love with me.

His name was Chuck Morgan. I learned through the grapevine that he was my age (six months younger, actually). He'd gotten his BA at UT, majoring in marketing, and had come back to get his master's degree in finance.

I told my roommates the potato story, and Stan said, "Wait, Chuck Morgan? I know that guy." Stan was getting an MBA too and had some classes with Chuck. Not only that, but Stan, Brian, and Chuck were in the same fraternity, Phi Gamma Delta, aka FIJI.

Brian said, "Do you like him?"

"No!" I said. "I don't like him, and I'm not dating."

"Does he like you?" he asked.

"He told me not to eat fat."

"He's a good guy," said Stan. "Really smart, just quiet."

"Yeah. If you're drunk and need someone to pick you up by the side of the road, you call Chuck Morgan," said Brian, who'd probably done exactly that.

Over the next two months, Chuck started to woo me like I'd never been wooed before.

The chase was on. Not that I knew it, because he didn't chat with me.

Instead of sweet talk, he did acts of service (what I learned was his love language) that I never asked him to do. Half the time, I didn't even know he'd done them. For instance, at the end of the night, everyone at the restaurant had to do side work, like refilling salt and pepper shakers. The worst job was cleaning the women's bathroom after a dinner shift. It was horrible, like a scene from *The Shining*. Blood on the walls, pee on the floor. Women are nasty. One night, I put on gloves, held my breath, and opened the bathroom door ... and found it sparkling and smelling like lavender.

One of my friends said, "I saw Chuck Morgan go in there earlier with a bucket and a mop." This man was so attracted to me that he scrubbed a toilet so I didn't have to. But I didn't care. I. Was. Not. Dating. Anyone.

During a break in my shift one night, I happened to compliment one of the other servers on her new purse. The next day, Chuck brought me a big Dooney & Bourke box with a ribbon on it and the same two-hundred-dollar handbag inside. The gift was too much. I didn't ask for it. It wasn't my birthday. If I accepted it, he would get the wrong idea.

I said, "Look, Chuck, I've been through a horrible marriage and a soul-crushing divorce. I'm really messed up, and I've got some things to work out."

"Okay," he said.

"You could chase me to Mars, and I still won't go out with you."

"Got it." In his mind, he probably thought, *She's been hurt. I can help her get over it. I'm going to make her change her mind.* "What about this purse?" he asked. "Should I take it back?"

I hesitated. It was a popular purse at the time. I hated to take an expensive gift from someone I wasn't dating. I didn't want to take advantage of him. But I really did want that purse. I decided to save him the chore of having to return it. (I still have it to this day.)

A few days later, Chuck overheard me tell someone I had a test in the morning and would have to stay up all night after my shift to study. He said, "I'll take your shift." It was ridiculous of him to even offer. I knew he was holding down two other jobs and attending classes.

"That's sweet, but I need the money," I said.

"I'll give you the money."

"I'm not doing that."

"It's no problem."

"Chuck, I told you. I'm not dating right now."

He said, "Okay."

My message was not received. Chuck kept chasing me.

He didn't like that I smoked, but if I ran out of cigarettes, he would drop whatever he was doing to go buy me a fresh pack. If I mentioned my love for big, cozy bathrobes, Chuck would show up at my apartment with a ribboned box from Victoria's Secret. He hand-delivered Bonnie Raitt's *Nick of Time* CD because he heard me singing "Have a Heart." I kept telling him my heart was not open for business, but he did not quit.

One night during a shift, I said, "I'm craving grilled shrimp." (You know how I feel about shrimp.) The next day, Chuck rolled a Weber grill several blocks to my apartment building, lit some charcoal, and grilled shrimp on the street for me. Stan, Brian, and their friends stampeded out the door to gobble them up. I held off on joining them to make a point. But that shrimp sure smelled good. I might've had one or two. Or ten.

I jokingly say Chuck stalked me. He was more of a lurker, always around, seeing to my every need, cleaning my apartment, washing my car. Doing and giving were his ways of telling me how he felt.

He was on fire for me. That was obvious. But I didn't get it. We had nothing in common (except for agreeing that I was too cute to clean). I liked to be the center of attention, and he was happy to stay in the background. I knew about movies, music, art, and cooking. He knew about math and practical stuff like how an engine worked and how to reconcile a checkbook.

"We're so different, I don't see how we'd get along in a relationship," I said to him at Grady's about two months after we met.

"Opposites attract," he replied.

THE CATCH

Nowadays the "catch" is when someone shares his contact info with you. With dating apps, people are too noncommittal to give their phone numbers. They just keep swiping, never committing. Back then, courting was more about getting to know someone's weaknesses.

One night, a couple with a baby came to have dinner at Grady's, and the baby started fussing. Chuck asked the mother, "Do you want me to hold your baby so you can eat?" He carried that baby around the restaurant for over an hour while he waited tables. Management thought it was sweet, and the grateful parents gave him a big tip.

Chuck loved a baby and was happy to hold one. But he did it for another reason. He knew my uterus was aching. I talked all the time about wanting a baby. So he made sure I saw him with a child in his arms to manipulate me.

It worked.

The next time he showed up at my apartment unannounced and started wiping down the shelves in my fridge, I said, "Okay, Chuck, I'll have dinner with you."

During that first dinner, he asked me, "Are we just friends or is this a date?"

I said, "It's a date."

I hadn't wanted to feel anything, but this man was reliable

and beloved by his friends. He proved to me that he was capable and considerate. It was only human nature for a woman to want to feel safe and protected. God made me that way! I could tell that Chuck was a hunter and a gatherer. No matter what, he could make a living. He wanted to do for me. If I was going to have a bunch of children, which I wanted to do, I needed someone who'd take care of me and them. I didn't need to stare into some man's eyes and then have my car repoed. (It's possible, after Evan, that my bar was low.) Besides, this man was going to chase me until he ran himself into the grave, and I didn't want to have his early death on my conscience.

So we started dating. It went well. About a month into our official relationship, while Chuck was mixing drinks behind the bar at Grady's, he said, "Three months from the day I get a good job, we're going to get married."

What in the world? I thought, *He can't be serious.* I just laughed it off and said something like, "Whatever you say, Chuck." Against my wiser angels, his proposal did make me feel alive again. I let myself imagine a future with him and liked what I saw.

THE KILL

Just a week after his spontaneous marriage proposal, Chuck said to me, "This isn't working for me. I want to break up." It came out of nowhere. I couldn't breathe. One day, it was "Let's get married!" Several days later, gut punch.

I was dumbfounded. I didn't think of Chuck as a chase-catch-kill type of guy, the kind who would lure you in and then dump you flat. There had to be another explanation. "I know you've been having a hard time lately," I said.

Chuck's job search wasn't working out the way he wanted.

Not his fault. This was during the elder Bush presidency and the first Gulf War. The economy was in a downturn, and businesses were scaling back on hiring people fresh out of grad school. Chuck got offers, but the salaries were in the same range as what he made before he got an MBA. When I asked about his search, he would change the subject, but I didn't realize just how rattled he was. He hid it well. Chuck's identity and sense of self-worth came from his work status. If he couldn't be the provider he wanted to be, then the whole relationship wasn't what he wanted it to be.

That's what I read into it when he said, "It's over." But his delivery shocked me. He was so cut-and-dried, with a blank expression like he didn't care. That was shocking and hurtful, from a man who'd promised he'd never hurt me.

"Why are you doing this?" I asked.

"Well, for one thing, I can't take the smell of cigarettes." That was the only explanation he gave me.

Young men can turn on a dime, and the relationship was over with no rhyme or reason to it. Chuck essentially gave me the "It's not you, it's your smoking" treatment. You'd think I would have started bawling or gotten mad at him for blindsiding me, but I went numb.

I quit my job at Grady's so I wouldn't have to see Chuck every night and got a new job at Lord Lindsey's in Knoxville. During my freshman and sophomore years, it was a Sodom and Gomorrah nightclub in an old antebellum mansion, with a black-and-white marble floor and good-looking bouncers. It was the place UT students went to dance and have fun. Thursday was Gay Night. On Saturdays, the place was popping. The DJ played Prince and Rick James. The actor David Keith, from *An Officer and a Gentleman,* was always there. I used to go to Lord Lindsey's to dance and flirt and have a ball.

The club had closed a couple of years earlier, and now Lord Lindsey's was a catering business for the well-to-do in eastern Tennessee. I was still a server. Same job, new venue.

Having latched on to my smoking as the reason Chuck dumped me, I decided to try the nicotine patch. The patch gave me horrible, vivid nightmares of somebody trying to kill me. And get a load of this: It caused flatulence. I had to walk through crowds of guests at weddings and bar mitzvahs holding a tray of stuffed mushrooms while emitting terrible gas. No one knew (I hope). I'm a southern woman. I hid it well. It's hard for me to even tell you all that! We don't talk about such things.

For a month, I didn't sleep. I was grieving. My hair was growing out horribly from the buzz cut. I was just a wreck. So I went back to smoking and everything got much better. I hate to even tell y'all that, but it's true. I'm so sorry!

Even in that pitiful state, some boys still wanted me. I rebounded with a long-haired blond boy, an artist. He painted big abstract pieces with hundreds of little squares. He was thin and wiry, and his whole wardrobe consisted of T-shirts, bike shorts, and paint-splattered tennis shoes. We met in the kitchen at Lord Lindsey's. One night, he picked me up at my apartment, and Brian said, "Either Lou's got a date or we're being robbed."

Except for his clothes, he kind of reminded me of my sister. The long-haired boy could make mayonnaise from scratch, and he danced like Michael Hutchence from INXS. And he was very forthcoming about his emotions. One day, we were riding in my car as always (he rode a bike with a sticker that said "Burn Fat, Not Oil"). He got really serious, grabbed my hand, and said, "If we get married, I want to stay home with the children, and you can make the living."

"That's so sweet," I said. "It's over. Get out of my car." What a turnoff! Even though I'd been burned by Chuck, I still wanted a man who would be a good provider.

To my surprise, I got over this breakup in record time. After just a month or two, I stopped crying to Patsy Cline and the Cure and started to feel good about myself. I had too much going on in my life to wallow. I was succeeding at college and taking care of myself financially. I had tons of friends and was closer than ever to my family. And I was nearing graduation, an incredible accomplishment for me. Not many people in my family had gone to college. I owed it to my parents, who'd supported me through one bad decision after another, not to fall apart. I just focused on myself and my well-being, and it worked. I was *fine*.

Six months after the breakup, I heard Chuck had moved out of Knoxville and was living in Bean Station, Tennessee, even more middle of nowhere than Adams. It's located in Grainger County at the foothills of the Appalachian Mountains, with precious people, beautiful lakes, and mountain views.

Apparently, Chuck and his daddy had been playing golf with some little old man named Fran who had a used mobile home refurbishing business. He wanted to sell that business so he could retire. Chuck Morgan decided to buy it.

In my head, I wished Chuck well in Bean Station, all by himself, with no one to keep him company but the women at the bank and the post office.

THE CRAWL BACK

Young women, know this: Every boy who dumps you is going to come crawling back. It might take a few months. It might take years. But one day, you will hear from him again—and by then, you probably won't want him.

A year after William broke up with me, he threw rocks at my apartment window, waking up my neighbors while he begged me to take him back. I ran into Evan on a plane twenty years after our divorce and finally got the apology I deserved.

Chuck and I hadn't spoken for about six months when I went to Key West for spring break my senior year with two couples, friends from Lord Lindsey's. I was the fifth wheel, but we had a ball. When I got back to Knoxville, I found out that Brian had hocked a lot of my stuff. On the plus side, I had a really nice tan.

I'd taken a second job at the Lancôme counter at the mall. I loved it, but those French words were really hard. My first day back after my vacation, I was straightening the stock of blush compacts and looked up to find a tall, freakishly thin customer standing at the counter.

"Hello, Leanne," said Chuck Morgan.

"What are you doing here?" I asked.

"I came to the mall to get a new shirt," he said.

He saw me first, so he could have run in the other direction to avoid a conversation. Instead, he made a beeline for me. And I knew why. I knew that hungry look in his eye all too well—and he wasn't hungry for cornbread. The look said he was tickled by the sight of me with a tan. He *longed* for me.

From that day on, he would not leave me alone. As I've told our kids many times, "Your very lives are based on the fact that your dad saw me with a tan."

He started calling me every night from Bean Station, and I tormented him for weeks by hanging up on him. He caught me in a generous mood one night, and I asked, "Will you come to my graduation ceremony? It would mean a lot to me."

"Well," he said, "I don't know if I have the time."

"Okay, butthole," I said, and hung up.

It was an unspoken ultimatum. If he came to graduation and spent the day with my parents, sister, aunts, uncle, and grand-parents, then I *might* consider taking him back.

Graduation day arrived, and Chuck showed up. He hung out with my family for hours. They all loved him. He was smart and responsible, the polar opposite of Evan. Mama was giddy with relief. Daddy looked at me and said, "He's a good one. This boy will take care of you." That was all he'd ever wanted for Beth and me. Uncle Raymond said, "Gal, you better hang on to him."

Chuck aside, graduation was a huge personal victory. It took me eight years on and off to get my diploma, and finally hold-ing it in my hand was more emotional and meaningful than I'd imagined. I had to overcome a lot of doubt and shame to start over again. But I did it. I was just so proud of myself. I wasn't going to let anyone or anything bring me down anymore.

A few months after graduation, Chuck said, "Marry me and move to the foothills of the Appalachians with me."

Has any woman in the history of the world received such a romantic proposal?

It wasn't the kind of proposal you read about in a novel. But I was happy to be asked. The part about moving to Bean Station worried me, though. I'd been through a lot, and the idea of being in a new place far from my family made me wary. But I agreed to marry him and relocate to the middle of nowhere. What can I say? I'd fallen in love with gifted-in-math Rifle-man.

Chuck was a shy introvert who didn't want a lot of attention, and I wasn't going to ask my parents to pay for another wed-ding, so we got married at the courthouse next to the copier. When Chuck put a ring on it, I thought, *I'm married to a hoop-dee-doo person. He has an MBA. He can reconcile a checkbook.*

There's no telling where we're going to go and what we're going to do! Chuck already had his own mobile home refurbishing business. With his brains and ambition, I knew he'd make it a success. I thought, *We're good.*

I was determined to make this marriage work. I was not going to be a two-time divorcée in my twenties (such an Erica Kane thing to do).

I had a bachelor's degree *and* a husband. Now all I needed was a few babies and a career in showbiz, and I'd be all set.

CHAPTER 6

What Every Newlywed Should Know Going In

Whenever people tell me their wedding day was the happiest day of their lives, I believe it. The marriage is all downhill from there—if you don't know what you've gotten yourself into, that is.

I'd never heard of premarital counseling until my son, Charlie, and his precious wife, Mary, went through it. It didn't mean there was anything wrong with their relationship. The point was not to peel back the layers of doo-doo from their past but to meet with someone smart and trained and talk about what was *really* important in their marriage. My son and daughter-in-law sorted out the practical, financial, and (covering my ears) sexual stuff ahead of time. Now they are in sync about everything, from who scrubs the toilet to when and where they take vacations.

I would have loved premarital counseling. Sitting on a nice couch and talking things to death? More fun than a day at Dollywood! But Chuck did not like to chat. Right from the start, Chuck Morgan and I were not that compatible. We're in sync about dogs and babies. But day to day, he's not a talker. In the six months we were engaged, we didn't have a single conversation about what our marriage was going to look like.

If we'd learned how to communicate and asked the right questions before our honeymoon year, we could have saved ourselves a lot of grief.

"Where Do You Want to Live?"

If someone asked me this typical premarital counseling question before I got married, I would have said, "In a nice house close to my family."

Chuck would have said, "Anywhere affordable."

We found our first home through Chuck's parents, Charles and Gail Morgan. They lived in Morristown, a medium-size town that has some fancy homes and a country club. Bean Station is like Morristown's rural country cousin. It has stunning lakes (and some fancy lake houses), but for the most part, it's farmland that families have worked for generations, with modest houses dotted throughout.

Some friends of Chuck's parents owned a lake house in Bean Station. "They have so many other homes," said Gail. "I don't think they darken the doors of that place." This little couple—precious, ordinary people you'd never guess were multimillionaires—were going to let us rent. And it was so cheap!

Chuck and I loaded all our possessions into boxes and drove to the lake house. My eyes popped when I saw it for the first time. We stopped at the bottom of the driveway to look at it, and I might have cried a single tear of joy. But then Chuck kept driving.

"Where are you going?"

"To our rental."

"It's back there," I said, pointing to the Barbie Dream Lake House behind us.

"We're renting the guesthouse. It's up here."

The guesthouse was off to the side by two hundred feet, but it was a world away in terms of comfort. It had two rooms with a couch, a bed, and a kitchenette, plus a tiny bathroom. When we walked in, I was hit by the musty smell of disuse. I wondered whether anyone had spent a night there before. It had a second-hand look, like whatever furniture the owners didn't want to trash, they stowed there. The walls were beige; the vibe was drab. My fantasies about being air-dropped into a hoop-dee-doo lifestyle dried right up.

As soon as we unloaded our moving boxes into the guest-house, Chuck said, "That's everything. I'm going to the office."

"What in the world? We just got here."

Chuck was a worker and had to get right back to it. He left me standing there in the beige bomb shelter and drove off. In his mind, he probably thought I'd approve of his devotion to work. I did appreciate that. But I was also completely alone in a new town, in a house that smelled like mildew.

"Are We Going to Be Spenders or Savers?"

My answer would have been, "I love to entertain and have nice things."

Chuck's answer? "We're not spending a dime on anything you don't need to survive." He's a good gift giver, but he's super tight with money.

So we moved into the dreary guesthouse, and I tried to be optimistic. The place had potential, but it cried out for sprucing. With a new rug and curtains, some throw pillows, artwork, and forty pillar candles, I could warm up the place. I made a list of things I wanted to buy and showed it to Chuck when he got home.

"We can't afford all that," he said. "We need to save."

"Save for what?" I asked.

"Retirement."

Lord, we were twenty-six! He acted like a sixty-year-old without a penny to his name.

I respected that Chuck was a saver. I'd probably be on food stamps by now if it weren't for him. His vacuum-sealed wallet reminded me of my father's, sort of. Daddy worried about saving for retirement too, but he still let us have some fun. He would drive us to the mall in Clarksville on weekends and let us buy lip gloss because he knew it made us happy.

Chuck Morgan took frugality to the next level. New curtains were out. I was limited to just ten pillar candles (I made a strong argument that I could not live without them).

Since I didn't know anyone, I didn't spend money on going out. Not that there was anywhere to go out to in Bean Station! Look, I was country. I grew up in a farming town where people didn't have much and there wasn't a lot to do. But Bean Station was something else. It had an IGA grocery store, a post office, Chuck's mobile home refurbishing business, a bank, a pharmacy, and a truck stop. That was it. The tiny town was one of Tennessee's oldest. It started as a frontier outpost at the foothills of the Appalachians, then home to two thousand people. I joked that it was like living in *Deliverance*. Adams was rural, but Nashville was nearby. Bean Station was rural, surrounded by more rural. My neighbors had never been to a big city. I'm not saying I was better than them or anyone. But I wasn't raised there, and I felt different from them. That was isolating. I need people. I need to chat.

It was a lonely time.

"What Kind of People Do You Want to Be Friends With?"

My answer: "Anyone who isn't a butthole to me."

Chuck's answer: "No time for friends. I've got a business to run."

For weeks at a time, the only people I talked to worked at Refurb Co., Chuck's business. His receptionist was named Pearl. He originally hired her to clean out the repossessed and previously owned mobile homes the company trafficked in. She'd had a baby as a teen, and her baby had a baby in her teens, which made Pearl a grandmother when she was in her late thirties. Now she was a fifty-year-old with a sweet spirit and a darling figure, just the cutest thing in a pair of jeans—and she was a great-grandma!

I loved Pearl and she loved me. I'd call her at work and ramble. She'd never had her own phone and it showed.

I'd call up and she'd say, "Hello." Not a question.

"It's Leanne."

"Okay."

"What are you doing?"

"I'm on the phone."

I'd monologue for a while. Finally, I'd say, "Well, I'll talk to you later."

"Okay."

It was like chatting with a child on a walkie-talkie. She didn't get the rhythm and etiquette. It took a while for her to learn when to hang up.

Pearl worked hard for Chuck and made extra money digging up ginseng in the mountains and selling it. She really loved Chuck. "When I started working here, I couldn't read a word," she once told me. "Never learned. Chuck told me I was smart, just uneducated. He asked me to answer calls and take down messages." He taught Pearl how to read and write phonetically. The key was to read her messages out loud so they made sense. I saw some of them, and they were like looking at the original Cracker Barrel menu, spelling "house" like "howz" or writing "n" for "and." I don't know what grade she got to in school, but she was sharp and a hard worker. She could have done anything, but she didn't have the chance. When I finally met her in person, I gave her a big hug. She was so tiny I could have squeezed her in two.

She was my only friend in Bean Station, and we talked for twenty, thirty, maybe forty minutes a day, before Chuck would ask her to get back to work and clean out a mobile home. I was a tiny bit jealous he had people around him all day. He spent more time with Pearl than he did with me. One day when I was fed up, I asked him, "Why do you take the time to teach Pearl to read when you could come home early and spend more time with me?" I was his new bride, all alone in a house with only ten pillar candles. I needed more!

He said, "Leanne, she has nothing."

Way to shut me up, Chuck.

I grumbled that my husband's fist was so tight. But the truth was, he knew the difference between having something and having absolutely nothing. In his mind, the only thing that separated us from Pearl was the grace of God. We had to save to be secure, to pay for our livelihood, and to make sure his employees had a steady living. He paid them better than he paid himself early on, and he deprived me of throw pillows. I resented it, but I understood.

"What Are Your Emotional Needs?"

My answer would have been: "My love language is words of affirmation. I need to hear you say that you think I'm pretty and that you love me every single day."

Chuck's answer? "I don't understand the question."

My husband was raised to have an old-fashioned concept of masculinity. If there was a terrorist attack, you wanted Chuck Morgan. He'd take charge, find food, break up fights. The man could change a tire, dig a hole, start a fire, kick a door in. But could he talk about his emotions? No. He couldn't read what people were feeling or understand people's sarcastic jokes (including mine). In his mind, it was his duty as a husband not to burden his wife with his doubt, anxiety, or sadness. Bottling up his feelings was one way he took care of me.

I got it, but I didn't like it! There had to be a middle ground between the overly emotional, long-haired, bike-riding artist boy who wanted to be my wife and Chuck, with his Fred Flintstone attitude about marriage and permanently plugged-up feelings.

He'd come home and I'd say, "How was your day?"

He was already talked out from dealing with people at work, so he'd give me just a few words, like, "I got the oil changed."

"Great," I'd say. "How are you feeling? What are your hopes and dreams?"

"About the oil change?"

"About life."

"I don't know."

"Well, let me tell you about my hopes and dreams."

He'd roll his eyes, telling me without words that he'd rather not listen to me. That didn't feel good. All I wanted was a little conversation. Some connection. Just half a dozen words of affirmation from him, and I would feel loved. Chuck didn't understand because he didn't have any emotional needs—but he sure had sexual ones!

"How Much Sex Do You Need?"

My answer? "However many times it takes to get me more pillar candles."

Chuck: "I don't need to talk about that." To this day, he just puts his hands over his ears and walks off. When we got married, he couldn't talk about it, but he wasn't shy to ask for it *without* words *a lot.*

I've often joked that I would love to be married to a gay man. I'd leave him alone; he'd leave me alone; we'd shop for fabric together. Instead, I married a big ole heterosexual with a lot of testosterone.

You never knew what would trigger him. I could be standing at the stove frying a chicken, and he'd come up behind me and grab one of my breasts. With all that hot grease popping, it was dangerous! I could be bent over, unloading warm towels from the dryer, and he would come up behind me and goose me in my butt thinking that would set me on fire. It did not. I could have been lying in a hospital bed with tubes coming out my nose, but if my paper gown parted and he spotted my doings, he'd push the tubes out of the way. He always wanted sex, but when he flared his nostrils in a certain way, I knew I was really in trouble.

I was aware of his big sexual appetite when I married him, and I made my peace with that. But I wasn't good to go at any moment. I needed to be warmed up first. Ideally, he'd say sweet things to me *throughout the day* if he wanted me anywhere close to being ready for contact. And with Chuck, all contact was sexual. It wasn't like he *ever* wanted to just hold my hand and give me a warm hug.

I asked him, "Can you touch me with it not being sexual? It

makes me feel like a prostitute when I haven't seen you all day, you don't say a word or hug me hello, and then you grab my boob."

He said, "_____." Nothing. He said nothing. He'd just sit on the couch, stretch out his long legs, and go on watching TV like an Appalachian Archie Bunker.

"How Involved Do You Want to Be with Your Extended Family?"

My answer would have been, "If we could live up each other's butts, visit every weekend, cook together, and have sleepovers, that'd be great."

Chuck would have said, "Boundaries!"

Everyone knows you don't just marry the man; you marry his family too. You see the in-laws on holidays and weekends, call them on the phone, get involved in their lives.

I had met Chuck's parents before we got married, and they were always very sweet to me, especially his daddy. Charles, who we called Papaw, was short and stout, played football and baseball in college, and had forearms like Popeye. He could have beaten the fire out of anybody well into his seventies, but that would've been out of character. He was just so bubbly and was loved by everyone. He got a kick out of me and loved my stories. When he had friends over, he'd say, "Hey, Leanne, tell them how your mama skins a deer with a golf ball."

Chuck's mama, Gail, was more reserved with me. I can't say I blamed her. From her perspective, her only son was ambitious, smart, tall, and handsome. He had an MBA and a bright future in business. He could have had anyone he wanted, and yet he chose me. She must have seen me as a troubled divorcée who barely got her degree. I think she knew I smoked cigarettes too. The thought of him marrying me probably scared her to death, as in, *What in the world is he doing with her?*

My best conversations with Gail were about Chuck. She lit up when I asked what he was like as a child. Apparently, he was brilliant, never gave her a minute's trouble, and loved PB and Js and basketball. In first grade, his teacher didn't give instructions well, and little Chuck came home and cried because he wanted to do well on his homework but didn't know how to. "He was beside himself," she said. "He wanted to be number one."

I learned more about the man I married from those conversations than I ever would have from Chuck himself. His intensity hadn't changed. If I asked him to plant a flower bed, he'd turn into Martha Stewart with a trowel. I said once, "I'd love a birdhouse in the yard." He didn't go buy a little wooden one you'd hang from a tree. He bought a ceramic birdbath on a pedestal and put a flowered border around it like someone had been buried there. And he dug a hole, cemented a long pole in it, and hung a bird mansion from it. It was a whole to-do. If I asked him to stop gardening and come in for dinner, he wouldn't even hear me.

The Morgan family dynamic was more aloof than the Fletchers'. In my family, we hugged and kissed one another on the mouth. I called Mama fifty-two times a day, and we said "I love you" a hundred times. The Morgans did not hug or say "I love you." They were loving people, but they weren't the type to say, "Y'all come over and have something to eat!" They were busy with their own lives, and we didn't see them too often, even though they lived one town over.

Meanwhile, my parents wanted to see me whenever they could. But they lived three hours away and had a business to run. When we did get together, well ... Chuck loved my family (and they loved him), but I could see how he'd need to go lock himself in a bathroom for an hour. We were a lot.

"How Clean Do We Want Our House to Be?"
My answer: "No one wants to live in a pigsty."

Chuck's answer: "Define pigsty."

I liked a clean house. Chuck liked a clean house. Our conflict was about what neatness looked like. For him, it meant spotless. He took after Gail, who was a local legend for keeping a museum-like atmosphere at home. Her house was beautiful—doilies everywhere, not a speck of dust. The rooms were so pristine you'd expect them to be cordoned off. In the dining room, where people served and ate food, Gail had white carpet. The carpet has been there over thirty years and still looks like it was put in today.

"Does anyone go in there?" I asked the first time I visited his family.

"What do you mean?" asked Chuck. "This is where we have dinner."

"And in all that time, no one spilled gravy?"

He shrugged. How would he know? He just lived there.

I was not raised to be obsessively neat. Lucille Fletcher's house looked lived in. My people would say, "It's strone." Good night, Lucille was busy working and raising us, so she let some things slide. Our house was never dirty, but it wasn't spotless either. A breakfast dish might sit in the sink for a while. Clothes were draped on chairs. You could find dust on the doodads. My sister took it upon herself to clean. Beth was very anal retentive and had allergies. "Someone has to get rid of all this dust," she'd say, and start fussing, cleaning, and sneezing while wearing a turban on her head, deep-conditioning her hair. I was no help. All I wanted to do was stay glued to Mom's side and tell her everything that happened to me at school that day. Beth would roll her eyes at my stories and crank the vacuum cleaner.

Mama, like me, was too fun to clean.

Chuck and I both took after our mothers, and my house-keeping skills caused a lot of tension between us. One night, after he complained about an unmade bed, I accused him of having unreasonable standards, and he said, "I don't expect it to be like my mom." That was a relief because if I lived to be two hundred years old, I'd never be as neat as Gail.

Our newlywed house was so small it felt cluttered if one thing was out of place. Untidiness had nowhere to hide. It was never dirty-dirty. The toilet sparkled, and I changed the sheets every week. The counters were cleaned but never cleared. I needed my things on top of them. Cookbooks. A coffee maker. A crockpot.

Chuck said, "Can't you store that stuff in cabinets?"

"I might need to make soup at a moment's notice," I said. "And you're not going to stop me."

Chuck once bought me an expensive vacuum cleaner. It was a marvel of modern invention. I loved it. I loved the idea of it. I just didn't love to use it.

A little bit of mess meant that a house was lived in, and I *lived* in my house. I wanted the guesthouse to feel like our *home*, a place where people would feel comfortable and want to hang out. Not a museum where they'd be scared to spill gravy.

For years, Chuck thought I sucked as a housekeeper, but we eventually came up with a fair division of labor: He was the provider. I birthed three babies and fed them from my body.

All the rest was not worth getting too worked up about.

CHAPTER 7

Storked

Get two or three mothers together, and before long, they will start swapping pregnancy and birthing stories. Men don't want to participate in this conversation because of all the blood and fluids and goo. They're too delicate and squeamish. If I said the word "cramp," Chuck would put his hands over his ears.

My grandmother Mary Lewis O'Neil (Lucille's mama) raised five children and gave birth to four, three of them at home. She once bragged to me, "When I had your mama, I didn't even take an aspirin tablet."

Every year on my birthday, Lucille tells me the story of my birth in exactly the same way: "It was a dark and dreary night. There was a cold spell, unusually cold for that time of year. It was spitting snow. Your daddy had cut meat all day and was tired. I went into labor and we drove to the hospital. Your daddy was out in the waiting room, sound asleep. I told the nurse, 'My baby's coming!' And she said, 'Your baby's not coming tonight.' She walked out the door and left me alone. I yelled to your daddy, 'Jim! Jim!' But he couldn't hear me. I could feel your head crown, so I put my feet up in the stirrups and had you all by myself." She was twenty-one at the time.

I had wanted to be a mama my whole life. When I was six, I put my baby doll next to me in Daddy's truck and pretended to drive to the store, flicking an imaginary cigarette out the window. So at twenty-seven when I became pregnant, I was thrilled.

I was working at Refurb Co. Chuck had opened a second location and needed me to answer the phone and talk to customers about the mobile homes we were selling. We'd moved into a cute townhouse in Morristown by then—and were getting to know some chatty neighbors—but I was still thrilled to get out and spend time in an office with people.

Sadly, the job didn't suit me. For one, Chuck was too busy to train his new (cute and fun) saleswoman. Lord, I had no idea what to say to those people on the phone! When they asked about prices or square footage, I just told them Chuck would call back with more information.

Then a family drove up in a Gremlin hatchback with the rear window out and a nine-year-old in the passenger seat smoking a cigarette. She lit it off her meemaw. I was country, but I had never seen anything like that. I quit smoking and the job that day, went home, and got pregnant that night. Turns out, I was as fertile as the Napa Valley. I could have had ten!

Back then, you had to wait two full weeks after your missed period to wee-wee on a stick. When I did it, I was alone in the bathroom. Seeing the pink plus sign appear in the little window was one of the happiest moments of my life. I couldn't wait to have a baby. I couldn't wait to have the company.

The thing about pregnancy: No one tells you what it's really like. They say, "It's beautiful" or "I glowed." Well, either those glowing people lied or I'm one of the unlucky ones. My pregnancy was not the hardest, but it wasn't the easiest either. I was so sick to my stomach the first trimester. The first day of the second trimester, I could have eaten a couch. I looked pretty normal until the fifth month, and then all of a sudden, people started asking me, "When are you due?"

There were two male doctors in the OB-GYN practice I went to. The first one was a smart aleck who made rude comments about my weight gain. "It looks like you're carrying twins," he said. "One in each butt cheek." He thought he was being funny, but I was so not laughing. The other doctor in the practice was precious Dr. Vick. Chuck and I were both crazy about him, and I was praying he'd be the one to deliver our baby.

The last trimester was by far the most painful. I had to sit on a doughnut-shaped pillow because my rectum hurt so bad. I'd read that pregnancy hemorrhoids were rough, but good night, this was agony. I could never get comfortable.

During those nauseated, rectum-bruising months, I thought a lot about the kind of mother I wanted to be, and it gave me an even greater love and appreciation for Lucille. She made everything fun. Adams was located in the heart of Dixie Alley, the eastern version of Tornado Alley, which put us in the path of multiple tornadoes a year. Mama loves storms. In another life, she should have been a TV weather person. She had a sixth sense about tornadoes, and whenever she saw the clouds coming in, she'd scoot us into the bathroom to wait it out. My sister would put her leg up on the sink so she could get close enough to the mirror to pop her zits. Mama would sit on the toilet and fire a Winston Light, calm as could be. I would stand in front of Mama, and we would just talk and talk until the storm passed. They were good times. She would keep the banter going and reassure us, "It's going to be okay." If I could be half as loving and fun as she was, I'd be a great mother.

Chuck's conception of time became clearer when I went into labor. It was the day before my due date, and I was as big as a house. For whatever reason, I started to crave pumpkin bread. I asked Chuck to go to the store and buy a can of pumpkin. I had the recipe card out and was ready to bake. I remember the dress I had on, a big floral number.

Food Lion was just a few miles away. Round trip, with shopping, the errand should have taken twenty minutes max. Half an hour went by. Then an hour. *Where is he?* I wondered. I could have made the bread and eaten it by now. I was watching *Wheel of Fortune* (which is bizarre because I hate a puzzle), and then my water broke. I knew what was happening because of the ten pregnancy books I'd read. I couldn't reach Chuck—this was before cell phones—so I called his mother, Gail. "I don't know where Chuck is," I said. "He was supposed to bring me a can of pumpkin, but that was two hours ago."

Gail said, "I'll be right over."

She was not the type to talk about personal things, but she was there for me when I needed her. I was alone, completely terrified, standing in a puddle of my own amniotic fluid. I spotted my mucus plug. I'd been waiting for that thing. That wasn't as fun as I thought it was going to be. But my mother-in-law showed up for me. She helped me calm down and change out of my clothes.

"Your water has definitely broken," she said. "This is it. You're going into labor."

Suddenly, the front door opened, and there stood Chuck. "What's Mom doing here?" he asked. His hands were empty.

"Where's my can of pumpkin?" I asked.

"Can of what?" he said. "Oh, I forgot. I stopped at Lowe's to look at chain saws. They're having a sale, and—"

"Chuck, Leanne's going into labor," said Gail.

"Do you still want the can of pumpkin, because I could run over to Food Lion now?"

"No! Lord, Chuck," I yelled. "I'm having contractions!"

"But you're not due until tomorrow," he said.

It never occurred to him that a baby could be born a day early.

I called sweet Dr. Vick, who said, "Stay at home. Make yourself as comfortable as you can and wait until the contractions are ten minutes apart."

Chuck agreed we should wait, so we did. I started timing my contractions. An hour went by, and the contractions hadn't sped up. Gail looked tired and said, "Well, the situation seems to be under control. I'll head home now. Call us when you get to the hospital."

Was it under control? Every two minutes, I said, "I think we should go now."

But Chuck said, "Let's wait."

Around 11:00 P.M., I was hurting pretty bad and my contractions were finally ten minutes apart. I said, "We are leaving *now.*"

We grabbed the to-go bag and left for the hospital. It was in Knoxville, fifty minutes away. I was scared to death I would have this baby in a car on the 11E highway. Chuck drove thirty miles an hour in a fifty-five zone. I assumed he was going slow to get us there safely, which was sweet. But this speed was ridiculous.

"Hurry up!" I yelled, grimacing during another hard contraction. "Why are you taking so long?"

Finally, the truth came out: "If we arrive at the hospital before midnight, they'll charge us for the whole day today. But if we get there after midnight, we'll only get charged for tomorrow."

What the ****, Chuck? If I could have killed him and still arrived at the hospital in time to have my baby, I would have done it.

We got there three minutes *after* midnight, much to Chuck's delight, and the hospital staff rushed me into a room to examine me. I was so relieved to get medical attention and to be around other people who would stop me from murdering my husband. But the excitement wasn't over, not by a long shot.

The nurse who examined me looked concerned. She said, "Your baby is breech and you'll have to have a C-section."

Breech! Why didn't we know that? I'd been going to the doctor every two weeks, and no one had said anything. I had a sudden flashback to a couple of weeks earlier. Chuck and I were sitting on the couch watching TV, and I was suddenly so uncomfortable. We looked down at my stomach. The baby's little fanny was poking out of my belly. It was either that or his head, a smooth bump you could see moving back and forth. It was the most bizarre, alien-like thing. I didn't know what was happening at the time, but I think that was when the baby flipped into the wrong position.

I burst out crying because it was so important to me to have a vaginal birth. I truly thought I was Mother Earth. I prided myself on how all-natural I was going to be as a mom. I pictured myself being like a mama gorilla with her baby, sleeping all cuddled up together. I believed in a family bed. I was going to nurse as long as I could. And I was going to have the best vaginal birth in history.

"Please, I know I can do it," I begged Dr. Vick when he arrived in the room.

"It's not possible," he said. "The baby is completely turned around. His feet are pushing on your cervix and rectum. I'm surprised you didn't feel that. It must have been very painful to sit down."

"I thought it was a hemorrhoid!"

"Not a hemorrhoid," he said. "The full weight of your baby has been resting on your rectum." So *that* was why I had to sit on a pillow for weeks. In my next two pregnancies, I had hemorrhoids galore, and they were *nothing* compared to what I went through with Charlie.

Postbirth, he has been nothing but an angel. As a baby, he was so sweet and would hold my bra strap and rub my back while he nursed. He'd smile at me and radiate a laid-back spirit. He was a yummy toddler and then a soulful boy who wanted to learn about wildlife and canning food. Prebirth, however, he was literally a huge pain in the butt.

The next thing I knew, they were wheeling me into the operating room. Chuck ran alongside the hospital bed and was there with me the whole time. They put up a sheet near my head so I couldn't see what was going on down below. I was awake for it all, though.

They numbed me so I didn't feel pain, but I still felt pressure. I thought I was going to vomit because I could sense them cutting and felt my innards tugging. It was the weirdest sensation. After opening me up, Dr. Vick took my uterus out and put it on my chest.

Chuck stood at my side and watched the operation. He barely spoke at all, until he said, "Your uterus looks like a Cornish hen."

Now I was really about to vomit.

One more weird tugging feeling, and Dr. Vick held up my beautiful baby for me to see over the sheet. "It's a boy!" he said.

And then a big, robust stream of urine arched out of my baby boy and sprayed all over the OR.

Chuck and I started weeping. We were just so overjoyed.

They put a little hat on the baby, who we named Charlie after his daddy and granddaddy, wrapped him up, and put him next to me so his face was close to mine. I looked right at him. It was just like looking at Chuck Morgan with a little mushroom cap on.

Seeing my son for the first time was supernatural. I felt God's presence in that room. Until that day, I was alone. And then I looked at my baby's face and knew what I was put on this planet to do. *This is it. This is why I'm here,* I thought. *I've waited for you all my life. I've known you all my life.* As I tell Charlie on his birthday every year, "My life started with you."

Dr. Vick was a wonderful doctor and surgeon. He sewed me back up so well that I was able to have two vaginal births after a Cesarean (VBAC). Usually, doctors don't let you even attempt a VBAC because it can be dangerous. I'm shocked that they let me try and that I'm still here in one piece. Without question or doubt, Charlie and his sisters, Maggie and Tess, are the best things that have ever happened to me. God blessed me with these precious children.

About ten years after Charlie was born, when we were living in San Antonio, Texas, Chuck and I went to marriage counseling, and the story of his dallying on the way to the hospital just to save a few dollars came up. Chuck grinned sheepishly to the therapist, precious Dr. Clifton, who I called Big Ole Doctor Clifton, and said, "Oh, Lord, I didn't do that."

But then he conceded that, yeah, he did drive slowly and prioritize the wrong things. And for the first time, in that room with Big Ole Clifton, Chuck apologized to me about his actions that night. He shared with me just how worried he was about supporting me and our baby, as well as his five employees. He was only twenty-seven years old, with the weight of the world on his shoulders. So busy at work, Chuck hadn't read all the pregnancy books that tell about every tiny thing that could go wrong. He just assumed we'd be okay. And, in the end, we were. It was such a huge step forward for Chuck to apologize and open up that I forgave him on the spot and let go of the last of my anger about it.

But do you see now why I had to become a comedian? I had to do something to cope with this man.

What I Didn't Know About Being a New Mother Until I Was One

It always annoyed me when people said, "Just you wait! You don't know what it's like to have a baby until you bring one home from the hospital!"

I thought it'd all come so naturally to me. I was wrong about that and about a bunch of other things. For instance, I had these foolish assumptions:

I'd wear my jeans home from the hospital. As it turned out, I had to wear my maternity clothes going home—and they weren't even baggy. It was devastating. I had no idea it takes a while for a woman's uterus to go back to normal. I felt mushy, so unattractive and swollen. I thought I'd strut out of the hospital looking like Farrah Fawcett, but I looked more like Dom DeLuise. I was like a baby elephant.

Nursing would be a snap. I thought it'd be instinctual, like a gorilla in the mist. But I had no idea what I was doing. I'd push Charlie's little face against my massive nipple, and he'd just cry. I had to work with lactation consultants. I fell in love with them. Thank God for those women. They not only taught me how to nurse but also shared their wisdom with me, like, "White baby boys are the laziest. They just fall asleep." I had no idea. They were right, though. Charlie would fall asleep, and I would have to tickle his chin and get him to open up wide to nurse. Fully awake, he was an overachiever at it.

Nursing wouldn't hurt. When Charlie started to latch on, it was like being stabbed with a knife. I felt like I needed to take a swig of whiskey and bite down on a stick, like when someone got shot on *Gunsmoke.* It took a long time for my nipples to toughen up, but once they did, I could have nursed everyone in Tennessee. I understand not everybody wants to do it or can do it. But I became really good at it. Between feedings, my milk built up so much that one squeeze could send it spraying across a room. I was so proud of that milk and of my body. I felt like Wonder Woman. Lynda Carter had nothing on me.

I'd be tired only for the first month or so. Chuck was working like a mule every day, so I wouldn't wake him up in the night when the baby cried. But after five months of feeling exhausted, you can get resentful when your husband just sleeps like a rock and never hears the baby. Chuck had these new Cole Haan loafers. Once at 3:00 A.M., I was so undone by exhaustion and annoyance, I thought, *I'm going to fill his loafers with breast milk,* and I did it. I sprayed it right into his shoes. He never knew it, though. They dried overnight. It was just my way of getting back at him. Anyway, I'm sorry I did it. Chuck loves a nice shoe. Lack of sleep can make you crazy.

Since I was home all day, I'd be able to keep a clean house. Being a stay-at-home mom, I thought, *I'm going to make this house spotless. I'm going to be Suzy Homemaker.* But I had to nap when Charlie napped. It wasn't a choice. I had to nap. So I didn't get anything done. The house was wrecked.

Dirty dishes, clothes, newspapers strone everywhere. It looked like a tornado went through it—and that was when I had just one little baby.

The baby would be all the company I needed. I fell madly in love up to my eyeballs with Charlie. But at the same time, as a new mom, my freedom was gone. That was hard to wrestle with. I know I was a good mama; I put all his needs first. But I was worn out and isolated. It was just me and him for hours on end. I fluctuated between feeling euphoric and lonesome. One minute, I'd feel like I didn't need anyone else. I remember thinking we could run off to California together. Then the next minute, I'd feel starved for adult conversation. It's not like Chuck ever chatted with me. And then I'd go back to thinking I wouldn't trade my time with Charlie for anything in the world. And I wouldn't. I'd go right back and do it all over again if I could, bleeding nipples and all.

CHAPTER 8

Going for the Gold (or Bladder Leaks and Selling Jewelry)

Becoming a mother is only the first decision you make. Then you have to choose what kind of mother you're going to be. A stay-at-home mother? A working mother? The whole "mommy wars" nonsense was heating up in the '90s when my children were born. And I thought it was stupid. Just be whatever kind of mother you want and need to be. The rest is nobody else's business.

It was never a debate for me. I wanted to be with Charlie. Chuck mentioned the idea of me going to work a couple of times, but I shut that down. I could not stand the thought. I felt sick to my stomach at the very idea of leaving the baby. You might as well have ripped my arm off. I could not be away from him. So I made a deal with my husband. "I won't get my hair done," I told him. "I won't put a picture on this wall. I'll do without. I won't spend any money. I have to be with the baby." And that was that. I didn't have one thin dime to myself, and I was okay with it.

Until I needed something.

I called Chuck one day and said, "We need a new dishwasher."

"No, we don't," he said. "I'll fix it."

A month went by, and he never touched the thing. I nagged him about not keeping his promise. I begged him to just let me buy a new machine. It wasn't entirely fair of me. I knew we were on a strict budget, and Chuck had a lot of responsibility on him. His philosophy was, "Make do. Don't spend money. Even if you suffer." Chuck believes in suffering. He really needs a therapist.

In all fairness to Chuck, when you run your own business, there are weeks when you spend all you've got paying everyone else and there's nothing left over for yourself. And nothing to give to your wife, even if she is willing to prostitute herself for a dishwasher. And I was! I would have done nasty, vulgar things for a new washer. But he would not budge.

That was when I realized that if I needed a little money, I was going to have to make my own. I needed a side hustle. As if God heard my thoughts, I got a call out of the blue from my old friend Alison (the one who let me sleep on her couch after my divorce). Since that dark time, she'd gotten married and moved back to Nashville. I was tickled to hear from her and so glad things were working out well in her life.

"Tell me everything," I said. "What do you have going on?"

"Leanne, I'm selling jewelry," she said. "It's like Tupperware. I have parties at people's houses and sell jewelry to the guests. You could do it too."

"How much are you making?" I asked.

She said a number that made me gasp. "Some women are making $150,000 a year."

I had never thought about doing anything like that before, but I could see the appeal. I could do the parties while Chuck took care of the baby at night. I'd make some money on the side for my hair and outfits for Charlie. It seemed like the perfect fit for me, so I looked into the company.

Premier Designs, out of Irving, Texas, was a direct sales jewelry business, founded in 1985 by a husband-and-wife team. The brochure said the company's ethos was to serve others and enrich people's lives, and who could argue with that? I got my hands on a catalogue. The merchandise was high-end costume stuff, and I liked it all right. I'd sold makeup and clothes before. I knew I could sell jewelry.

Here's how it worked: I had to buy a starter kit of samples in a big case with stackable black velvet jewelry trays. Then I would book parties at people's houses and display all the samples on a table. The guests would pick through the samples and then place orders for the pieces they liked. Their orders would then be mailed directly to them. So all I would ever have to schlep around was the samples case. The incentive for the woman hosting the party was a bunch of free jewelry.

It seemed like a sure thing. Even during wartime, women will buy lipstick. Most of the items were in the twenty-dollar range. If the guests were having a good time, they'd buy more than one item.

I knew from working at the Clinique counter and waiting tables that laughter is like wallet lubrication. If you made sure people were having fun, they'd spend more. And they'd be more likely to book their own parties, where I could sell more jewelry. If I could make it fun, women would go wild. The hosts— stay-at-home moms, mainly—would have an excuse to throw a party for their friends, and they'd get some free jewelry too.

Right now, you are probably thinking, *Don't do it, Leanne! It's a scam or a cult like that leggings company LuLaRoe! It's going to destroy your life!*

Premier Designs was a multilevel marketing company, what

some might think of as a pyramid scheme. But the company was always on the up-and-up to me. The owners seemed like sweet, upstanding people. Alison assured me the business was legit. Honestly, I didn't know to be wary about it or to ask questions. I just thought, *This could work for me.* Alison recruited me because she knew I could sell and a portion of my profit would go to her. If I went into this business, I was supposed to line up other people to work under me too.

I wasn't so keen about managing other people. With a baby at home, it was all I could do to manage myself—to do the laundry, make dinner, and take a shower every day. I wasn't a natural leader or business brain. Balancing a checkbook and delegating work were not gifts of mine. But I was up for dazzling and flinging jewelry at parties, making money all on my own. Now that office work was out, it would give me a new social outlet.

RETURN OF THE QUESO DIP

For my first party with the company, I was told to invite everyone I knew to my house. Once my guests saw how great the merchandise was and how fun the party was, hopefully they would book parties at their own houses. Then I'd cart my case over there and start earning a commission. For my kickoff party, I invited Beth, Mama, and some women from my little church—and they all said yes.

That was when I got nervous. It wasn't enough to put the velvet trays on the table and say, "Have at it, ladies." I had to do a sales pitch about the jewelry and the company. I'd been tickled by the idea of dazzling, but now I had stage fright. I hadn't spoken in front of people in years. And I was a new mother, not back to pre-pregnancy weight. If Charlie cried when I was doing my presentation, my milk might let down and I'd soak my shirt in the middle of the talk. More important, what if they didn't like my queso dip?

The party was on a Saturday afternoon on a hot summer day. About half an hour before the guests were supposed to arrive, I asked Chuck to go down to the Pilot gas station at the end of the road and get some ice.

He said, "In a minute."

"The guests will be here soon, and I don't want to serve them warm tea."

"I just need to finish one thing."

This again.

In those final minutes before the guests arrived, I was so busy setting up and nursing the baby that I didn't realize Chuck had taken the front door off the house to saw an inch off the bottom. It was lying in the front yard when people came, and the women in their pretty dresses and heels had to skirt the door to get inside. I couldn't believe it. *Why now? What in the world?*

I could hear people saying, "Is this place still under construction?"

Chuck never did get the ice. (He'd been in the process of renovating the house and had laid the hardwood floor the day before. And he'd just discovered the door wouldn't open because of the added height. "I had to do something!" he said. He could have told me that at the time. Lord!)

I welcomed the guests and asked them to have a seat for a quick presentation. I really wanted to impress these women so I could get started in this business and also so they would like me. I was so nervous, I thought I was going to vomit and have diarrhea at the same time. I wore a denim shirt with a southwestern cactus pattern, and I pitted out big rings of sweat on my blouse. I started with the script they gave me, saying, "Thank you so much for coming! I want to show you some beautiful—"

Just as I started talking, a deafening whirring sound came from outside, right through the open doorway of the house. Chuck had started the lawn mower and was riding it around the yard. We didn't have curtains, so everyone could see him through the windows as he made circles around the house. I think Chuck was nervous for me and was coping by doing stuff in the yard. Whenever he was nervous, he did chores. If we were invited to people's houses for social gatherings, Chuck went straight to the kitchen and started cleaning the toaster until it looked brand-new out of the box. He cleaned like he was the event planner. People used to say to me, "I've never had any housekeeper as good as Chuck." I think some invited us to parties because they knew their fridge needed a cleanout.

The entire time I was trying to get the guests' attention, they were staring at my husband and making side glances at one another, like, *What's he doing out there?* I had to shout over the lawn mower. He cut the motor as I was screaming my last sentence, and some of the ladies began to cover their ears.

I'm going to kill him, I thought.

Thankfully, my guests didn't flee through our open doorway. They stayed for warm tea, ate some dip, and pawed through the necklaces and earrings I'd laid out on the coffee table. Despite the rocky start, the day was a success. Several of the women set up parties of their own, and I was in business.

MY SECRET WEAPON

The company gave me a script to use at the sales parties that said things like, "Add chandelier earrings to an outfit to go from day to night!" It didn't really hold the ladies' attention, and they bought only one bracelet, or the cheapest necklace, just to be polite.

I wasn't supposed to go off script, but one day, I dropped the usual pitch about how a clip-on earring can change the look of a pump and started telling personal stories about being pregnant and taking care of a newborn. I just threw out random stuff about my hemorrhoids, or breastfeeding at Walmart while a little old man stared at me and ate his hot dog, or how I wanted to kill Chuck because he never seemed to hear the baby cry at night. Many of the ladies had little babies, and before long, we were all laughing about our selectively deaf husbands and our thoughts of murdering them.

As telling stories became my party schtick, my sales took off. The events were less about selling merchandise and more about a bunch of moms having a good time at a hilarious group therapy session. I felt like I was putting on a show. "You can either see me in Las Vegas later or have a party with me now," I said at the end of my presentation. And sure enough, I got new bookings at every party. Random strangers who'd heard about me from a friend of a friend called to ask me to come to their house "to perform" . . . and to bring some jewelry too.

Is this it? I wondered. *Is comedy my way into showbiz?* I'd grown up watching *The Tonight Show* and loved it when Johnny Carson had stand-up comics on to perform. My jewelry patter was sort of like stand-up comedy, but it wasn't a string of jokes with a setup and punch line. I told stories about my life that developed into an act. I ad-libbed and brought the audience into it. Whatever you wanted to call what I was doing, people loved it. And I was making a few hundred dollars per party that I could spend on the baby and my highlights.

I MADE A GROWN WOMAN PEE HERSELF

I did one party at the home of a woman I met at the country club in Morristown. I loved her whole friend group, including Carmen, a darling woman who now works at my eye doctor's office.

At that party, I told a story about my second pregnancy with Maggie. "My hemorrhoids were so swollen, they were hanging out of my butthole," I said. "My doctor, Dr. Otis, was a darling older man from the Methodist church, with a second wife and a second family. He came to the office on his day off because I cried on the phone, and he had to bring his little five-year-old boy, Ben, with him. So Dr. Otis had me lie on my belly on the table and pointed this bright light on my hemorrhoids so he could—I don't know what he did, cut them off with a hot knife? Anyway, his tiny child kept trying to get in front of him and look at my butthole. I couldn't see what was going on, but Dr. Otis kept saying, 'Ben, get out of the way. Ben, stop staring. Ben, you're blocking my light.'" (That kid is probably a surgeon now.)

Carmen, seated on the end of a couch, laughed so hard at my story that she spit out her lemonade. Then she said, "Oh gosh, I'm so sorry! I peed on the couch!"

The host went to get a kitchen towel and started blotting.

Meanwhile, I was thinking, *I'm killing it. I made Carmen pee herself.* When I saw the stain on the couch, I knew I really had something.

I look back at that as a God moment, one of those times when He pointed me in a new direction. Carmen was just one woman. If I could make a whole room—a whole theater—full of people do that, I might be able to do comedy for real and get paid for it. I've since told Carmen, "You don't know what your accident meant to me. It was a defining moment in my life." I just love that doll. Every time I go to the eye doctor, we hold each other.

THE PREMIER EVENT OF THE YEAR

One year, Premier Designs held a regional conference in Nashville, with speakers and entertainment. Word reached the upper echelons of the company that a woman in east Tennessee was booking parties months in advance, and they wanted me to be a speaker. I was flattered they'd even heard about me, let alone asked to me to get up onstage in front of three hundred people to talk about the secret of my success.

If you've seen the docuseries about LuLaRoe, and how weird and cultish their conferences were, put that out of your mind. The Premier Designs regional conference was nothing like that. Distributors weren't forced to go or spend a ton of money there. It was just a gathering of women at the Opryland Resort, an opportunity to take some classes and get fired up about their businesses.

Adams was only thirty-five miles from Nashville, so Lucille met me there. I brought Charlie and Maggie with me. Right before I was supposed to go on, I went into the bathroom, sat down on the toilet, pulled my dress up, and nursed Maggie. Lucille wanted to watch my talk, but we decided she should sit in the lobby with the kids in case they got fussy.

I was wearing a long sweaterdress that was not fitted. The color wasn't flattering, but I never spend my money on myself and hadn't thought to buy a new dress. I thought this taupe thing would hide my still-bloated figure, like throwing a blanket over an elephant.

I waited off to the side, nervous, in terror of vomiting, until the MC said my name. Me and my stretched-out dress went out there. I was supposed to talk about how to book parties, but I couldn't tell these women, "The secret is to basically do stand-up in living rooms like it's a comedy club."

So I walked up to the podium, not quite sure what I was going to say. I could see the audience, hundreds of women in rows of plastic chairs in a huge room with a high ceiling and bright lights. They put a lapel microphone on me. I'd never been miked before. I opened with, "Hello, it's great to be here. I might seem a little drained because I just breastfed my baby on the toilet and handed her off to my mama."

I got a solid laugh, and I was off to the races from there: spraying milk; little Ben and my hemorrhoids; dozing off in a rocking chair and waking up trying to breastfeed a lamp; asking Chuck to watch Charlie when I was sick, Chuck going the whole day without feeding him or changing his diaper, and my thinking, *I'm never going to have a moment's peace for the rest of my life.* The laughs got louder and louder. In that room, I could make eye contact with those darling women, and I just had a ball.

When I walked off the stage, I didn't think, *That was all right* or *I didn't humiliate myself.* I floated off, knowing I just killed.

It's hard to describe the feeling of killing onstage. It's like you're plugged into the sun. Like any worry you've ever had disappears. Doubts and anxiety come back, believe me. But for a few minutes, you feel bulletproof. It's like riding the perfect wave. Everything's clicking and you can't do wrong. Not that I've ever surfed! But I love those documentaries about surfing boys.

Premier Designs had hired a comedian named Dennis Swanberg for the conference's entertainment. Dennis performed at all the big churches and was beloved in the Christian community. He came up to me as soon as I got off the stage and said, "You are so funny! You *need* to be a stand-up!"

That was another God moment. Dennis, a professional, was telling me, a mama with two babies in the foothills of the Appalachians, that I could be a professional comedian too. In all my thirty years, I'd never personally met anybody who did this for a living. So hearing Dennis say "You need to be a stand-up" just blew me away.

The one time in my life that I'd been to a comedy club was in Los Angeles before Chuck and I got married. We'd gone to California for a vacation to see my sister in Huntington Beach. Chuck asked me, "What do you want to do in Hollywood the most?"

"Go to a comedy club," I replied, no hesitation. "And go on the Grave Line tour." It was my dearest wish, having flown across the country, to see where famous people died.

In the afternoon, we did the murder tour—"We put death on the map!"—and were chauffeured around in an actual hearse to famous sites like the Charles Manson murder houses, the Beverly Hills mansion where Bugsy Siegel was shot, the apartment building where Jack Cassidy burned to death, and the alley where Sal Mineo was stabbed. Chuck thought it was morbid. But I loved this stuff.

That night, we stood in line at a legendary club, the Comedy Store, to see a great lineup, including Dom Irrera and Paul Mooney. The young girl who served our drinks had a southern accent. "Where are you from?" I asked.

"Alabama," she said.

"Are you in L.A. to be an actress?"

"I'm trying to do stand-up."

When she said that, my heart started beating out of my body. If she thought it was possible, and she worked at the Comedy

Store, then maybe it was. As I watched the comedians onstage, I had this deep, physical reaction that I can hardly explain. I just thought, *I could do this. I'm supposed to be doing this. I need to do this.*

Years later, at the jewelry convention, Dennis Swanberg stood in front of me, repeating and validating those inner thoughts.

I had no idea hosting that first party would eventually lead to my thinking I had a future in stand-up. But it did, and it changed my life.

Even as I fantasized about performing in places like the Comedy Store, I knew this dream wasn't practical. There weren't any comedy clubs where I could go to open mike after I put my babies to sleep. Still, I started to believe in myself.

But meanwhile, it was back to spit-up, poop, diaper cream, and sleep deprivation.

As God Is My Witness, I Will Never Play Volleyball Again!

On the weekends, Chuck played in a recreational basketball league. While I changed diapers, he shot hoops. That didn't sit right with me.

So I decided to sign up for my own sports league, tickled by the idea of showing off my athleticism to Chuck. He knew I was on the starting lineup on three teams in high school, but he'd never seen me in action. I went with volleyball because my milk-heavy breasts were as big as basketballs. There's no way I could have run up and down the court.

I arrived at the high school gym on a Saturday morning, ready to dazzle, with Chuck and the baby in his stroller. Everyone who signed up was divided into teams. My team had no idea they were about to be dumbstruck by my volleyball skills.

The other team served first. The ball came across the net and was bumped by one of my teammates, a perfect setup for me to spike the ball over the net and win the point.

I bent my knees to leap into the air . . . and barely got off the ground. My vertical was half an inch. I looked down at my legs, wondering how somebody had managed to pour concrete into them. I swung at the ball and completely whiffed. My breasts got jostled, and two circles of milk immediately soaked through my T-shirt. My face must have turned red because the woman next to me asked, "Are you okay?"

No, I was not okay! I was beyond embarrassed! I glanced into the stands and saw Chuck sitting with Charlie. He waved at me and gave me a thumbs-up, the butthole.

I finished the game, but I was pitiful. I blamed nursing. I was weighed down by the gallons of milk I carried around wherever I went. Or maybe my athletic ability had been sucked out of my body through my nipples. Breastfeeding was much more important to me than sports, so I made my choice and never played volleyball again. Amazingly, I haven't missed it.

CHAPTER 9

Double-Wide

When you hear, "Your life is about to change!" you probably think it means something good is coming. No one thinks, *Oh, Lord, things are about to turn upside down!* But sometimes, what you think is going to be great turns out to be horrible. And what you think is going to be horrible winds up being a blessing in disguise. You just can't know how things are going to play out in the end.

Okay, philosophy sermon over. I'm just setting up the story of some of my family's most chaotic years, when we had about as much change—good, bad, and crazy—as we could handle. We moved four times in five years, and let me tell you, nothing will test a marriage like moving. Here's what I learned.

WHEN YOUR HUSBAND SAYS "DON'T WORRY," IT MIGHT BE TIME TO WORRY

Out of the blue, Chuck made an announcement: His dad was going to take over Refurb Co. because Chuck wanted to try something new. He wanted to move to Myrtle Beach, South Carolina, to help open up a NASCAR-themed café.

I had two babies in diapers, and he dropped this on me like a bomb. He never asked for my input. By his logic, he was doing me a favor by not burdening me with these decisions.

What in the world, Chuck? I was livid. My brain hadn't exited my body along with my second baby.

He said, "Don't worry, Leanne. I got this."

After a crazy week of packing for the third time in three years, we moved to a new state where I didn't know a soul. "It's just temporary," Chuck assured me. Our cute little house was in the old part of town that tourists avoided. It was just a lot of retirees, and us. Every day, I loaded my babies in their double stroller for a long walk on the beach. We played in the sand, soaked up the sun, and took in the ocean air. The house was small enough that it didn't wear me out to take care of it.

Working at the NASCAR café, however, didn't play out as Chuck had expected. He had to be there eighty hours a week, and the people he worked with were typical hard-partying res-taurant types. It wasn't a good fit for a family man, and it wasn't the life we wanted. He had to pivot and got a part-time sales job at a department store while studying for the LSAT. He loved education and learning and was seriously considering law school. He would have been a great lawyer. He was stubborn and com-petitive and, Lord, did he love to argue and fuss. While he was deciding what to do, I started working at the same department store, a flashback to my college days at Miller's. His shift began when mine ended. We'd hand off the babies in the parking lot.

This time, I was a perfume spritzer. I was not, and never had been, a fragrance lover, especially after nursing. Whenever I spritzed some Shalimar on a shopper's wrist, I got an instant headache.

I was so exhausted all the time that I thought, *Oh my Lord, am I pregnant again?* So one day, I took Charlie, age three, and Maggie, age one, to Walmart to get a pregnancy test. The kids and I went into the bathroom at Walmart together, and I peed on the test stick.

Charlie took one look at my face and, deadpan, said, "Is it positive?"

It was. I drove home and called Chuck. "I'm pregnant again," I said. "I'm going to walk out in the woods and let the animals eat me."

Here's the thing about Chuck Morgan: If he needed to dig ditches or drive a truck to provide for his family, he'd do it. He'd work harder than anyone and end up owning the company. The department store noticed how smart he was, so they asked him to go into management. He turned them down and rejected offers from a few prestigious law schools too.

He had a better offer. A big manufactured-home retail company was looking for a salesman. Chuck got the job, so we moved right back to the same town we'd just left the year before. I was thrilled to return to my friends and church in Morristown and to be closer to my parents.

I asked Chuck, "Where are we going to live?"

He said, "I'll take care of it. Don't worry, Leanne."

Immediately, I started worrying my head off.

DON'T JUDGE A HOME BY THE CINDER BLOCKS IT'S SITTING ON

We moved back to Morristown but we still didn't have a place to live. We were staying with Chuck's parents, and that wasn't an ideal situation. One night while I was feeding the kids their dinner, Chuck cleared his throat to make another one of his life-changing announcements. I braced myself against the kitchen counter. *Here it comes,* I thought. *Pray for me!*

"Dad has a double-wide for us at Refurb Co.," he said.

"A *what*?" I shook my head, not getting it.

"It's a bargain because it was repossessed by the bank."

In my mind, living in a repossessed manufactured home was a step down, like we'd fallen on hard times. A year ago when we lived in Morristown, I'd been a member of a local country club. And now I was pregnant and going to live in a repo. Not good.

Some of the homes that arrived at Refurb Co. were not what you'd call "gently used." When tenants got evicted, they sometimes took out their anger on the homes they were forced to leave. They might bash out the windows with a hammer or trash the kitchen.

"What's wrong with it?" I asked.

Chuck shrugged, his way of downplaying something bad. "Someone set fire to it," he said. "But it's been all fixed up. It's in good shape now. We're going to put in a foundation, set it up, and live in it for a while before we flip it."

"Hold on, Chuck, you already *bought* this mobile home?"

"A double-wide," he said. "I promise you, Leanne, when we resell it, we'll make money. It's just temporary."

I would come to learn the double-wide was set up on a quarter-acre lot in the middle of a field. There were half a dozen other manufactured homes on other small lots, but it wasn't a park with a neighborhood feel. The grass was overgrown. There were no paved paths between the houses, just a gravel strip on the side of the main road.

Once again, Chuck never asked for my opinion. He thought not telling me about important stuff made him a good husband

and provider. In reality, it made me a furious wife. Being married to Chuck was like being in a dark room and not being able to find the doorknob.

I knew that Chuck Morgan could make a living off a flat rock. His own father told me before we got married, "You better watch Chuck. He'll bury money in the backyard like a squirrel." I had no problem with that. But his squirreling away information felt like he didn't respect or trust me. I'd put up with a lot from him. The moves . . . His grabbing my breasts day and night . . . I deserved more than this.

When we drove out to see the house for the first time, I was exhausted and not in the best mood. The house was set on blocks, about three feet off the ground, but it did not have steps to the back door. I would have to throw my little babies up in there. Then I had to climb up. I was pregnant, a double-wide myself. I had to hoist one leg up into the doorway and, using all my strength, heave the rest of me up to get inside.

I was expecting the worst, but honestly, it wasn't bad. You could tell there had been a fire because there was still a faint smoky smell. But it had a lot of rooms—four bedrooms, three bathrooms, an open-plan living room. The kitchen was clean, but the sink was tiny.

Right before we moved in, Mom and Dad came for a visit, and they tried to be positive. Mama said, "The layout is so nice and open."

Daddy said, "You could ride a bicycle through here."

"Thanks for saying that," I replied, "but we're living in a hole."

My pride had gotten to me. Have you seen manufactured homes lately? Unbelievable! They would blow you away. They're beautiful! Hardwood. Marble. Back then in a repo? Not so much . . .

Our neighbors out there were sweet, though. One of them

had a potbellied pig that huffed and charged at me like a snorting little bull whenever I left the house. I'd have to scramble to get away from it. I was scared to death of that thing. It was so tiny, the size of a small dog, and it couldn't have done much damage to me. But still, why come after me? Did he hate pregnant women? How bizarre! And how did that thing always escape from his pen?

We all need to be humbled by life sometimes and appreciate what we have. I just wasn't used to being chased by pigs and having to roll my pregnant body up into the doorway because we had no steps.

Meanwhile, Princess Diana died in a car crash in Paris. That made me cry for a week. I was never a royal watcher, but that tragedy triggered feelings of helplessness in me that were lurking just below the surface. Right around then, Beth had gotten married to a wealthy man. I was happy for her, and a little jealous. Her life seemed so much easier than mine, and it brought back the sad comparison I used to make when we were in college. My sister had her act together; I was flailing and lost.

I'd stopped doing jewelry parties, but I was hosting a nonstop pity party in my own head. And I was the only one who showed up.

GOOD NEIGHBORS WILL ALWAYS GIVE YOU A LIFT

We lived between two worlds. We had our wealthy country club friends from before we moved to Myrtle Beach, and then there were the good old blue-collar neighbors who lived on our road.

I can't say which group I liked more. At a holiday cocktail party with the Junior Reading Circle, a charity group, one woman, very hoop-dee-doo in her designer dress and heels, said in front of a bunch of people, "Hey, Leanne, are you still living in that trailer park?"

My heart just sank. She must have seen the shock on my face because she quickly said, "I'm sorry. I shouldn't have said that."

I told her it was okay and headed for the bathroom. I was leaning against the pedestal sink with fancy perfumed soaps in a dish. (Fragrance—hate it!) They made me sneeze and simultaneously wet myself.

And I just cried. I thought, *My life is over. I have no control over my body. I have no control over anything.*

I wasn't upset because I thought I was too good for a manufactured home. I was living in one, so how could I be too good for it? That woman's comment was meant to humiliate me in public. She was just so mean, kicking a pregnant woman while she was down.

Most of our friends understood our living situation. That woman reminded me that you can have all the money in the world and still be a butthole.

Our neighbors took a liking to me, but most of them were confused about our family's situation. Chuck had a good job, and yet we lived in the middle of nowhere. We were super frugal, but I drove an Infiniti sedan we had bought years earlier. These people were very helpful with advice. One old man who always wore the same dungarees watched me throw my two babies in through the back door of the house and then heave my swollen self in after them. He pointed at my pregnant belly and said, "Don't you know what causes that?"

I said, "Yes, I do. But I need the money." I'll be honest, I had prostituted myself to Chuck Morgan for luxuries like Stride Rite shoes.

Anyway, that shut him up.

Another neighbor named Judy was a forty-something chain

smoker. She would walk into our place without knocking or being invited, smoke her generic cigarettes, and drop f-bombs like daisies. Judy was married to Bob, a frail fifty-year-old who smoked cigarettes while he was on oxygen. They had a precious teenage daughter named Savannah. They let Savannah's boyfriend move in with them, and no matter what he was wearing or doing, you could see his hairy butt crack.

Every Wednesday night, our church held a worship service with a meal afterward. I never missed it. I got to see our friends, I didn't have to cook, and the kids could play. It was the one thing I looked forward to every week. One Wednesday, I accidentally locked myself out of my house with my car keys inside. I wanted to go to that church service so bad, so I walked down the road holding Charlie's hand and with Maggie on my hip. I asked Judy to give me and the kids a ride to Chuck's office and to stop first at our place to get the car seats from my unlocked car. The floorboard under the passenger seat of her car was rusted out, so I could see the highway under my feet as we drove. My two babies were in the back. I glanced at them and saw Charlie holding Maggie's hand. Charlie, smiling, said to Judy, "Nice car you got there."

Judy smoked and complained the whole way about Savannah's boyfriend who "clogged our f*%$ toilet after eating two f*%$ boxes of mac 'n' cheese, and my husband on oxygen had to get out the f*%$ plunger and unclog it." She was real sweet.

I remember looking out the window, swallowing hard because the cigarettes were making me sick, wondering if my two babies were inhaling the smoke, and thinking, *What in the world, God? How did I get here?*

And, as sure as I'm sitting here typing these words, I felt in my spirit that God spoke to me. He said, *Just wait, Leanne. There's a reason. Just hold on. This will all make sense to you later.*

I've got you in the palm of My hand. I've got a plan. It's already in motion.

The way I interpreted God's message was that this incident, and that whole year, were just part of my story. They were a chapter in my life, and that chapter wouldn't last forever. My story would go on and change, and all I had to do was sit back and wait for my life to unfold. I felt a peace come over me. *It's going to be all right,* I thought.

We pulled up to Chuck's office. When he came out and saw the condition of the car we were in, he grabbed his chest like he was going to have a heart attack. He was embarrassed that I couldn't reach him, stuck out there in that field without a cell phone and dependent on Judy to rescue me. He was also probably scared because he knew I'd blame him.

That was a turning point for him. He looked at me and said, "Okay. We'll move."

UNPACKING BOXES INDUCES LABOR

True to his word, Chuck flipped that manufactured home for a big profit, and we bought a new house in a neighborhood in Morristown called Magnolia Pond. The house was a new construction, what you'd call a starter home, a good size for a family: three bedrooms, two and a half baths, and a big yard.

After seven months in the field, we moved for the fourth time into what felt like our new old life. Our church community came through for us on moving day. My Sunday school friends, some who were pregnant themselves, helped us pack things up, and their husbands did all the heavy lifting. I was about to burst, so I didn't have to carry anything bigger than Maggie. We were so grateful for their help. Some of them are still our dearest, oldest friends.

I was induced exactly one week after we unpacked at our new house. While I was birthing Tess, Chuck was supposed to hold one of my legs, but he was on his cell trying to sell a home. Lucille was in the delivery room with us. Mama was a loyal Chuck fan, but with him on the phone and my leg just flopping around, she shot him a horrible look and said to me, "You need to get your tubes tied."

Chuck got his priorities straight and put the phone in the crook of his shoulder. He kept talking while holding my leg and managed not to drop the bag of popcorn in his other hand. I smelled that popcorn during the entire delivery, and it made me sick. To this day, the smell of popcorn—and generic cigarettes—makes me gag.

We brought Tess home and settled into Magnolia Pond with joy, relief, and a sense of having survived something. And I was determined to rewrite some rules for our marriage. Chuck was going to stop keeping me in the dark about major decisions. He was going to ask me for my opinion about things that affected all of us. Bottom line: Wherever we lived—a nice house or a manufactured home—didn't matter. I just wanted to feel like I had a say in how our lives played out.

SAVANNAH'S BIG DAY

I kept in touch with Judy for a spell and brought her leftover food from our church's Wednesday dinner night, just to make sure that Kraft mac 'n' cheese wasn't the only food her family ever ate.

When Tess was about two months old, Judy greeted me at her door and said, "Leanne! Savannah is pregnant. We just found out! I don't know how it happened."

"You don't?" I asked. I didn't say, *Well, you let her boyfriend move in.* "How far along is she?" I assumed she was three months or so.

"She's due next week," said Judy.

What in the world?

They threw Savannah a baby shower at Burger King. Talk about awkward. Burger King was buzzing. A few maintenance guys were cleaning out the ball pit because a child got sick in there. People came and went on their lunch break. Judy didn't book the space—can you do that at Burger King?—so we were crammed into two tables. No decorations at all.

I brought a gift basket with glass bottles, rubber nipples, onesies, baby wipes, and spit-up cloths. The gathering was small, just a few neighbors from the road, including the potbellied pig's mom. The only man there was Bob with his oxygen tank. (The boyfriend with his hairy butt crack wasn't allowed.) We had Whoppers—I love a Whopper Jr—and toasted to Savannah and the baby's health with Coca-Cola. And then we went our separate ways, into our futures. I never saw them again.

I still think about Savannah's baby, Bob's oxygen, and Judy's salty mouth sometimes. I hope that they're doing well out there somewhere and that the boyfriend stepped up as a dad and found pants that fit.

My darling Uncle Raymond in a tobacco field, 1949. He believed I could make it in Hollywood (specifically, doing Vanna White's job).

My beautiful mama, Lucille, with her Brigitte Bardot hair topper, 1969. I loved that thing.

My precious step-granddaddy, Frank Valenzuela, and grandmama, Emma, 1970.

Me at Ellen's Beauty Shop getting a shampoo and set, drinking a Coca-Cola, 1971.

Me and my "frail" sister, Beth, at the Lodge at Paris Landing, Tennessee, 1974. We would give anything to be that frail now.

Sports meant everything to me and then I found boys, 1979.

Lying in the sun, tense, thinking somebody might honk, 1980. Copperheads probably close by.

Robertson County Fairest of the Fair pageant, 1981. I made one wrong turn and got cut. Always the bridesmaid, never the bride.

Li'l Abner play, Jo Byrns High School, Cedar Hill, Tennessee, 1983. I was Stupefyin' Jones.

Beth was Homecoming Queen at Austin Peay State University when I was a freshman at the University of Tennessee in 1983. Look at our hair!

Look at that Chuck Morgan in love with me in 1991!

Premier Jewelry National Convention, 1995.

All Saints Episcopal School, 1999. Where did the time go?

First time doing stand-up in Morristown, Tennessee, 1999.

My first grandbaby is born, 2020.

My beautiful family at my grandbaby's baptism, 2021.

My family onstage at my Netflix taping in Lexington, Kentucky, 2022.

PHOTO: JOSEPH LLANES

Brian Dorfman, my dear friend
and cheerleader! The Ryman
Auditorium, Nashville,
Tennessee, 2023.

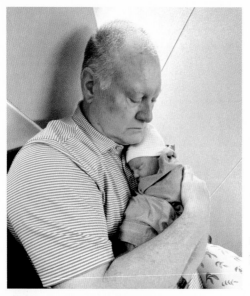

Our second grandson is born, 2023.

Austin City Limits Live at the Moody Theater, 2023. Two sold-out shows, with my "Little K" Karen Mills opening. A dream come true.

PHOTO: TROY CONRAD

CHAPTER 10

What's Wrong with Being Confident?

When your last child stops feeding off your body and can get her own juice box, you start to wonder, *Is this it? Is life just going to be one day after another of me trying to figure out what I'm supposed to be doing with myself?*

I loved being a mom. Taking care of my three babies was the most important thing to me. Being their mama was enough. But I always had this tug to perform and entertain.

When Tess went to Mom's Day Out at church and I was finally able to crawl out from under a mountain of diapers and see daylight, I didn't know what to do with my free time. I joked with friends that I might start drinking whiskey and going honky-tonking like those tacky women who leave their kids in bed to barhop and whirl their purses in the air at nightclubs.

That didn't happen. Nothing did. I thought I'd have all this freedom, but I spent most of Mom's Day Out running errands and doing chores before it was time to pick Tess up, put Maggie down for a nap, and take Charlie to T-ball or the dentist.

Life was still a grind. When Chuck asked me to get a part-time job again, I said, "How? I'm in the car for five hours a day!"

But I felt like something in my life had to change. Two things, actually.

I GOT NEW BREASTS

After nursing three babies, my breasts were concave. Each one looked like an M&M in the bottom of a tube sock. I couldn't get an A-cup bra to fit right. The bras I had kept riding up because I didn't have boobs to hold them in place. I remember being in church in my nursing bra and a white turtleneck sweater. The bra migrated up until its two padded cups were wrapped around my neck. I couldn't pull it down in church. People would notice and talk. Here I was, singing "The Old Rugged Cross" while two cones were poking out of my collar bones. And I had to just sit there.

I might have had a bit of body dysmorphia, thinking I looked much worse than I actually did. But I did feel terrible about myself. I was only thirty-three. I still had a lot of life in me left, and I didn't want to feel painfully unattractive.

So I got implants. Beth didn't think it was a good idea. She said, "I don't want you to look tacky in tube tops." Did she think I was going to do a wet T-shirt car wash? Tacky how? This was never clarified.

I said, "I promise not to use my implants for evil."

In a different conversation, Daddy said, "Why would you want to do that to yourself?"

Mom told him, "Jim, she needs to." Lucille had seen me without clothes on. She knew the situation was dire.

Good Lord, I just wanted to feel like a normal woman again

and fit into my clothes. To have boobs instead of socks on my chest. Plus, I needed them to balance out my big butt. I'd always had junk in the trunk, but after three pregnancies, my butt went global. I could hold up a cafeteria tray on my fanny. My kids liked to play with it, but only in public.

Things would get stuck in my butt crack. If I stood up at church, Chuck, the stoic, would calmly turn to me and say, "Leanne, get your dress out of your crack." It made me furious.

"Leave me alone, Chuck," I'd say. "If my dress is in my crack, it's none of your business."

My implant surgery went fine. Sweet Lucille came to stay and help me as I recovered from getting "those big blown-up things," as she called them. I didn't care what people thought. I felt good in my clothes again, and my new breasts definitely made me feel better about myself.

TRY THE ROAST BEEF!

Within a month of my surgery, a friend from Sunday school class, a Kiwanis member, found me at church and said, "We need somebody to MC a cabaret night/variety show we're putting on to raise money for charity. Would you be inter—"

"I'd love to!" I said.

The variety show was at the high school gym. I MCed the heck out it and loved doing it.

A man in the audience came up to me afterward and said, "I own a sandwich shop on Main Street right here in Morristown. There's a little stage in the front. I have bands play on the weekend, and I was wondering if you'd consider—"

"I'd love to!"

Mike the Sandwich Guy and I worked out a deal. I would do an hour-long set. He would promote it and charge a cover price.

The door money would be all mine, and he'd make his profit from the extra beer and sandwich sales the live performance would bring in.

My entire experience doing stand-up comedy was those jewelry parties. Five years had gone by. Would the same stories kill at a sandwich shop? And did I have enough material to fill an entire hour?

At home, I would do the dishes, dry off my hands, take out a notepad Charlie used in kindergarten to practice writing his ABCs, and make a list of things I could talk about onstage:

- Ben and the hemorrhoids
- The black hair that grew out of my belly when I was pregnant with Charlie
- Wanting to bite down on a stick while breastfeeding
- Wanting to kill Chuck (an evergreen)

That was the extent of my preparations. I was too busy being a mom to practice in front of the mirror. I was excited about performing and anticipated feeling the same rush I got at jewelry parties and that regional sales convention.

Then again, what if I wasn't nearly as funny as I thought I was? I might make a fool of myself in front of all my friends and neighbors. The nerves kicked in, and I was on the verge of throwing up for days.

Chuck drove me crazy about a lot of things, but the night before the gig, he told me, "Leanne, you'll be brilliant." And then he flared his nostrils at me, and I had to fake having irritable bowel syndrome.

When I woke up in agony the next morning, I wasn't faking. I couldn't move my neck. I begged my way into an emergency appointment with an ear, nose, and throat doctor, convinced (and terrified) that something was seriously wrong with me. He looked just like Tim McGraw.

The doctor examined me and said, "I don't see anything."

"I can't move my neck, and I've got this big performance tonight," I said.

"Aha!" he replied. "Maybe that's it. You're scared stiff."

Still suffering, I got my hair done at a walk-in chain, and it came out looking like a helmet. I was sure the show was going to be a disaster. I told Chuck, "Don't you dare come by! Stay home with the kids."

When I arrived at the sandwich shop, Mike told me they had a full house. Either everyone in town had nothing better to do, or they were fascinated by what I might say—or curious to see me fall flat on my face.

The room *was* crowded. Each metal chair around the dozen or so café tables was occupied by someone I knew or recognized. Everyone seemed happy enough, drinking soda and beer, scarfing impressive-looking sandwiches that came out of the kitchen at a steady flow. I had zero appetite. The smell of French dip wasn't helping my nausea.

Mike led me through the tables to a little riser in front of a big picture window that faced the street. It was hardly a stage at all. My neck throbbed as I stepped up there. I was so scared I thought I was going to faint. *Just get it over with,* I told myself. I picked up the microphone and started talking.

Once I opened my mouth, something unbelievable happened. My neck pain dissolved. My muscles relaxed because it felt *right* to be up there.

I didn't have confidence before I got on the stage. But being up there filled me with it. There was a big lesson in there somewhere, something along the lines of "take the first step and the path will appear," but I was having too much fun talking about hemorrhoids to dwell on it.

During the set, I spotted through that big picture window Chuck driving up and down Main Street a few times in the minivan with those babies in the back seat, all of them waving at me. He had to do it. He was worried about me!

The audience didn't choke on their roast beef from laughing while they ate, but they did get on their feet and applaud with gusto when I finished and took a bow. I felt a warm glow inside. It was my Sally Field moment. They liked me; they really, really liked me. It felt *good*.

And I wanted to do it again and again.

As soon as I got off the stage, Mike rushed over, handed me three hundred dollars, and said, "You were amazing! Do you want to come back next week?"

Lord, yes. A thousand times, yes.

ALL THIS AND CAFETERIA FOOD TOO!

I thought my career might begin and end at Mike's Sandwich Shop on Main Street in Morristown. But word spread, and I started getting asked to perform at other places around town. Most comedians work their act out at open mike nights at comedy clubs. I was doing it at the Kiwanis hall, the sandwich shop, and the Rotary club. I would drop my baby at Mom's Day Out, do an hour here and there, and make a little bit of money. Not much, but enough to buy myself a top and things for the kids.

An eighty-year-old woman at my church who volunteered at the local hospital asked, "Would you come and do something for the volunteers? We'll pay you with a tray of cafeteria food."

Of course I would! I liked performing for those sweet people, and I always loved cafeteria food. Who doesn't love a meatloaf and a blue Jell-O?

And they loved my jokes. "With my first baby," I told them, "I was so exhausted, I'd sit in a rocking chair with him at my chest, look out the window at the people, and wonder, *Where's she going with lipstick on?*" I told the story about working at Chuck's office in Bean Station, and the Gremlin driving up with the nine-year-old smoking a cigarette that she lit off her meemaw.

Making people laugh made me feel like I was contributing to the greater good. It was also just plain fun. I loved getting a laugh and the bulletproof feeling of confidence it brought on.

Not only that, but stand-up gave me something to look forward to. It gave me an identity that was all mine, apart from being Chuck's wife or my babies' mama. I treasured the years of staying home with my children and wouldn't trade them for anything. But comedy allowed me to connect with myself and other people. As an extrovert, I really needed that.

THE REAL DEAL

The nearest comedy club was an hour away in Knoxville, and I was fairly certain they did not have an on-site babysitter. It would be inconvenient, but getting onstage at a real club in front of paying customers would boost my confidence to the stratosphere.

I resolved to call at least one club, just to see what happened. The biggest venue in Tennessee that I knew of was Zanies in Nashville. It was close enough to my parents that I could leave the kids with them while I drove there to perform.

I had to work up my nerve to pick up the phone, telling myself over and over that the worst they could do was say no. My palms sweat while I punched in the numbers, and when a man answered the phone, I nearly hung up. I took a deep breath and said, "Hello! I'm Leanne Morgan. Who are you?"

"Brian Dorfman," he said. I had no idea I was talking to one of the most powerful people in the comedy business. Good thing, or I might've fainted.

"I'm just wondering if I could come by one night and do a set for y'all."

Brian laughed. Good start!

"Have you ever performed comedy before?" he asked.

"I can send you my resume. I kill weekly at Mike's Sandwich Shop. I have them rolling in the aisles at the Rotary."

"Is that so?"

"It is very much so."

Brian paused, and my heart stopped beating. He was actually considering letting me perform. Finally, he said, "I never ever do this, but, okay, Leanne Morgan. We have a spot for an opener next week. I'll give you ten minutes."

"Thank you, Brian! I'll be there!" I was thrilled and scared and overwhelmed and couldn't believe it.

Another rule about confidence: It gives you the courage to ask for what you want. And by the grace of God, you get it. And what did I want more than anything?

MY FIRST *REAL* COMEDY GIG!

Around a full year after my first appearance at Mike's, I drove to Adams and parked my babies with Lucille. Then I drove to Zanies. The place was dimly lit and cavernous, with several well-stocked bars, a balcony with cocktail tables, and, in the main room, up to fifty long tables, all of them angled toward the stage—a real stage, with hardwood flooring and a spotlight.

I expected to find a brick wall behind the stage—the classic backdrop for a stand-up routine—but Zanies had a shimmering blue curtain that would be flattering to my skin tone.

That Wednesday night, the place wasn't packed, but the audience was bigger than any I'd had before. I was opening, meaning I went on first, followed by a feature act and, finally, the headliner, Billy Gardell. Billy would go on to star in the sitcom *Mike & Molly* with Melissa McCarthy.

Beth and her husband, Lawson, promised to come and lend their emotional support. I spotted them at a table in front and went right over to them. My big sister gave me a tight hug. "I'm sick to my stomach and scared to death," she said. "This is going to kill me." My sister takes on the pressure of everything I do, like my mom. She feels every show I've ever done out of love and protectiveness. If people didn't laugh, she might stand up in the middle of my set and tell them off.

I found the backstage area and was guided by the club manager to stand in the wings and wait to be announced. My legs and hands were shaking from nerves. Of course I was rattled! Confident or not, it was my first professional stand-up club gig. Zanies was the real deal. This was *it*, the biggest thing that had ever happened to me. I might as well have been headlining in Las Vegas.

As nervous as I was, I still knew this was what I was supposed to be doing. It might sound weird that I was quaking in my kitten heels while also being certain I'd kill. But I'm a woman. I can feel two different, even contradictory, emotions at the same time—and they're both real.

I went out there and did my thing. I can't remember what I said exactly, but it was a shortened version of my sandwich shop routine about nipples and hemorrhoids. It wasn't polished. I had no idea if you could call it a set, but I didn't care. I just gave it a whirl until the light on the stage apron flashed, which meant my ten minutes were up. I thought it went well.

On pure adrenaline, I floated off the stage and back out onto the floor to find my sister. Beth gave me a hug and said, "You were great, Leanne! I got through it."

Brian Dorfman was very busy but generously offered to sit down with me in his office and talk for a long time. "Leanne, I think you got something," he said. "To make it in this business, you have to be on the road working every week. But you've got three babies to raise. There's a reason you don't see a lot of moms doing comedy. It's just too hard."

I took Brian's words to heart. He had been in the comedy world for years. He clearly knew what it would take to make it. I had no reason not to believe him. I listened and nodded along. I didn't get angry or scared. But I remember thinking, *I hear you. I get what you're saying. But I know I have something. I'll figure it out. I'll find a way.*

I wasn't going to put my aspirations in front of my children. The most important thing to me was to raise them and put them first. If clubs weren't possible for me, I'd go elsewhere, like I'd been doing. I realized I was probably naïve to be so confident, but then again, I had a stable home life with a husband who supported my doing comedy. I had great material. And I had these "big blown-up things." What could possibly stop me?

How to Survive a Long-Distance Marriage

Chuck turned out to be a genius at selling manufactured homes. He rose like a rocket in his new company, and they wanted him to oversee all of Arizona and part of New Mexico.

We went on a trip out west to check out the city of Phoenix.

I really liked it. The houses were nifty. I love a good stucco with a tile roof. I shopped for turquoise and silver jewelry and enjoyed the dry heat and citrus trees. Was the guarantee of good hair and fresh lemons worth moving across the country and leaving everything and everyone I loved behind? Absolutely. At that point, my biggest adventure was the seven months we spent living in the double-wide. I was excited to get out of Morristown, Tennessee, and go somewhere new and bigger. And the desert was beautiful.

We put our house on the market, with every intention of moving to the Land of No Frizz. Meanwhile, Chuck had to start work in Phoenix and flew home every three or four weeks. For the next eight months, I barely saw my husband. I had three babies under five and was taking care of them by myself, *and* I had to keep the house clean because potential buyers were coming to look at it. How did I survive this?

God-like patience. Chuck would call after a steak dinner with coworkers and ask, "How are you?"

I'd say, "I haven't showered in a week, the place is a mess, and we have three showings in the morning. I'm doing just wonderful."

Lax fashion choices. I wore the same three pairs of gray sweatpants and white T-shirts for a year straight. The elastic waistbands helped me. I gained weight because I had time to eat only packaged food. Meanwhile, Chuck went on the Sugar Busters diet and lost twenty pounds. Another reason to want to kill him.

Reinforcements. People asked me who I missed more, my husband or my mama. I answered, "My mama! She knows how to wash a plate. And she talks."

Lucille drove three and a half hours from Adams to help me whenever she could. She always said "It's going to be okay" to my face. But she had her doubts. I overheard her talking to Daddy on the phone during one of her visits. "I don't know how Leanne's going to do it," she said. "It would take three women and two men to run this household."

I thought, *Lord, if Lucille doesn't think I can do it, I'm screwed!*

Sacrifice. To save my marriage, I had to kill my comedy career so I could be home at night with the kids. I wasn't thrilled about it, but I used Chuck's catchphrase, "It's just temporary!" And it was. I picked up comedy again a year later.

CHAPTER 11

Burning Love

One time-honored tradition for American families is the road trip.

The Fletchers didn't travel much because sides of beef weren't going to butcher themselves. But before Daddy built the meat processing plant, we went on a road trip in 1968, when I was three.

Like any good Tennessee family, our number one destination was Memphis.

Our first stop was the Memphis Zoo, the biggest in the state. I remember being really excited to look at animals I'd seen only in picture books. Nowadays, zoo animals live in habitats that are designed to remind them of the Serengeti or the Congo, but in the late 1960s, the animals were kept in sad cages. Beth and I ran up to the chimpanzees, three or four of them in a big cage with steel bars they could swing on.

Mama said, "Don't get too close, girls."

"What are they doing?" asked Daddy, peering through the bars.

The biggest chimp was holding something, and as we watched, he wound up and threw it through the cage at us like a baseball. A pile of it landed right by my feet.

"Doo-doo!" I screamed.

"Run!" yelled Daddy.

Mama picked me up in one arm and Beth in the other and sprinted away from the chimpanzees, which were now lined up at the front of the cage, whipping hot feces at people. Lord, they could *throw*. No one in our family got hit. We got lucky that day.

From the zoo, we drove to Graceland, the fourteen acres of farmland that Elvis bought in 1957 for himself, his parents, and his grandmama Minnie Mae. In 1967, Elvis's bride, Priscilla, moved into the mansion on that property. Ten months later, they welcomed their baby girl, Lisa Marie. When my family visited, Lisa Marie was about three or four months old.

Being from Tennessee, we thought of Elvis as ours. When outsiders made fun of him—for his weirdly close relationship with his mama, the rumor that he stopped having sex with his wife after she gave birth to their daughter, or how heavy he got later in life—we couldn't stand it. They had no right.

We joined the crowd of fans standing on the sidewalk in front of the gates to Graceland. The steel gates fascinated me. They were very tall and decorated with musical notes and two outlines of Elvis playing guitar.

My mama was determined to see Elvis and Priscilla. She wasn't shy about that kind of thing. One time, when we saw the Osmonds in concert, people were standing up and dancing right in front of us and we couldn't see a thing. Lucille threw a red-and-white box of popcorn at the head of the woman in front of us and snapped, "Sit down!" Daddy looked like he wanted to crawl into a hole, but Mama didn't flinch. She was just happy it worked. For herself, she'd never do that kind of thing. But for us, she'd proudly throw popcorn or an anvil so Beth and I had a better view of Donny and his brothers. I get it. It's an animal instinct. A powerful feeling comes over you, and you'd fight a tank with a machete to help your kids. Lucille let her mama bear come out of the cage.

At Graceland, I was too young to understand exactly why we were standing on the sidewalk in the hot sun for an hour, but I knew it was important to my mama to be there. I was also too small to really see anything, not that much was going on.

And then the crowd started to stir with excitement, pushing forward to get closer to the gates. I noticed a man on the other side walking toward us down the long paved driveway.

"Someone's coming!" said Mama.

"I want to see!" I whined.

Lucille picked me up and put me on her shoulders. I could finally see the elegant white mansion with Grecian columns in front and the rolling green pasture behind it. As the man got closer, the crowd grew even more tickled.

Mama said, "Oh gosh, y'all. It's Vernon Presley!"

He came right up to the gate and said, "I'm sorry, folks. Elvis and Priscilla are here today riding horses and we can't let you come any closer."

Right at that moment, I noticed two bobbing heads with coal-black hair on horses in the distant pasture. As a child, I remember feeling awed that I caught a glimpse of the couple all these people had come to see. The moment stayed with me.

And then something happened that, according to Mama, sealed my destiny.

Vernon Presley, a doll, came through the gates to talk to fans.

He smiled right at me and said to Lucille, "Isn't she the cutest little trick?" Mama lowered me to the ground, and Elvis's daddy touched me on the head.

To Lucille, it was like a blessing, a holy moment. "Elvis's daddy touched you!" she said, her voice hushed reverently for the rest of the trip. When she tells this story now, she always says, "That touch from Vernon Presley is why things are happening for Leanne now." I don't know whether she really believes that or if it's for dramatic effect. Maybe a touch from Elvis's father did have something to do with my success? Who can really say why any one person is struck by lightning, or a TCB lightning bolt?

THE DAY ELVIS DIED

I barely remember our road trip to Graceland, but I'll never forget the day Elvis died, which was a trip in and of itself. It was August 1977, and I was almost twelve by then. Beth and I found Mama crying in the kitchen. On TV, a news anchor from a local station was visibly shaken, talking about Elvis's life while pictures of the King flashed in the background.

"Elvis is dead," said Mama. Beth hugged her, and they started sobbing into each other's arms.

How could Elvis be dead? He was just a few years older than Daddy. Lucille, Beth, and I watched TV as more information came out. At first, there was a lot of confusion about how he died. People were saying he overdosed on pills or had a heart attack or choked on a fried peanut butter and banana sandwich. It came out later that he had a heart attack on the toilet while straining to poop and—this is heartbreaking—wasn't found for hours. He was always constipated because of all the uppers and downers he took. Bless his precious heart.

From that day on, I became obsessed with eating fiber. I've always been constipated myself, but not because of dope. I also took note that fame and riches don't protect you from loneliness and tragedy. Good to know, since I was going to be a star one day.

THE MORGANS TAKE OVER GRACELAND

In 1998, we were on the move again. Chuck had gotten another promotion, and we were moving to San Antonio.

We decided to road-trip from our current home in Morristown to our new one in Texas, a mere 1,165 miles away. The kids were seven, five, and three. (You might be pulling your hair out just imagining this nightmare.)

Seventeen hours in a car is a pain in the butt for anyone (where was my blow-up doughnut pillow when I needed it?), but having to manage three children in the back seat of a minivan was going to be torture for me. No one had iPads back then, so the little ones had no distractions. They cried over every tiny thing. And there was an extra layer of anxiety because Maggie threw up anytime she got in a car. I kept a Walmart sack ready for her to puke in.

It was a miserable trip. Five people shared one bottle of water. Chuck wanted to drive straight through, no stops, so we weren't allowed to pee or empty that Walmart sack. A few hours in, I managed to doze off, and was awakened when Chuck screamed, "When did you last get the oil changed?" The check oil light had come on and he was furious. I wonder if the stress of that trip gave me shingles.

I insisted that we stretch our legs every three or four hours. "Let's stop at Graceland," I said. "That'll be fun." I was the same age as Tess when Vernon Presley touched my head. Would the place look the same as my faint memories of it? I was excited to find out.

Chuck Morgan had our route planned to the millisecond, and he was not enthusiastic about going to Graceland. But I pulled out the big guns. "We're stopping at Graceland, or I'll never do it with you again."

He said, "If you don't take care of my needs, I'm getting a girlfriend."

"That's fine. Just make sure she's stout and can mow because I need the help." He rolled his eyes.

Then I turned to the kids in the back seat and said, "Guess what? We're going to Graceland!" I clapped and bounced in the passenger seat, trying to drum up some excitement from them to compensate for their daddy's being a butthole.

"Yay!" they yelled.

Charlie asked, "What's Graceland?"

"It's where Elvis Presley lived."

"We're going to see Elvis?" asked Charlie.

"Well, no, he's dead. He died a long time ago."

"And they let people visit his house and look at his stuff?" he asked.

"It sounds strange," I admitted. "It's like going to see where George Washington or Thomas Jefferson lived. They were two of our first few presidents. You can tour their houses too."

"Was Elvis a president?" asked Maggie.

"No," I said. "But he was the King."

That impressed the kids. "Mama, how did Elvis die?" asked Maggie.

I was so tired that I just blurted out the truth. "He had a heart attack because he was straining really hard while trying to go to the bathroom," I said.

My kids have told me over the years about some other inappropriate things I said when I was too rattled and tired to see straight. For example, when Charlie was in middle school and we had the birds-and-the-bees chat, he asked, "How many times have you and Dad done it? Three times?"

I said, "Well, whenever I needed grocery money."

I shouldn't have told Maggie how Elvis died. She was the type to immediately start thinking, *Oh my gosh, what if I strain to poop? Am I going to die?* Like mother, like daughter. She did look a bit horrified. As if trying to find the bright side, she asked, "Is Elvis in heaven?"

"He was very spiritual and a strong believer, so yes," I said.

"Is Johnny Cash going to heaven?" Somehow, she knew the singer had had some troubles in his life.

I turned to Chuck. "A little help?"

He said, "We can stay at Graceland for an hour, tops."

Sighing, I said to Maggie, "You know what? I think so. I think Johnny Cash loves the Lord and is going to be in heaven."

"Is J.Lo going to heaven?" she asked.

"I don't know." How horrible of me! It was another one of those exhausted-mom blurts.

Thank God we got to Graceland because I was exhausted from having to pronounce judgment on the souls of celebrities.

My first impression of Graceland as an adult: The house was a lot smaller than I remembered. As a child, I thought it looked like the White House. Now I realized it wasn't much bigger than a nicer-than-average home in Nashville. From the outside, it was even kind of plain. You'd think Elvis would have lived in a much fancier house. That shocked me.

The tour guide was a darling little woman who I could have put in my pocket. She gave us headphones with prerecorded narration about the house and its history with the King. I would have loved to experience the entire multihour program, but

Chuck did not have patience and was dreading the drive. I also missed a lot of the recording because I was wrestling three children and trying to keep them from running off.

When we walked into the living room, the recording played the opening notes to *2001: A Space Odyssey,* followed by one of Elvis's more up-tempo tunes. Maggie and Tess started dancing, and the other people on the tour glared at us. They'd traveled from all over the world to be there. This tour was a big deal to them. So when my girls were going nuts, no one else thought they were as cute as I did. I would have loved to dance too, but we probably would have gotten kicked out.

We spotted a roped-off bathroom. Maggie stared at the toilet inside and asked very loudly, "Mama, is that where Elvis died?"

I said, "I don't know, but let's keep going."

"Tess, Charlie, come look at the toilet," she said. My three children stood at the velvet rope, staring at the toilet for I don't know how long. The other tourists were sneering at us while I smiled apologetically.

Chuck yelled, "Let's go, let's go. Enough staring at the toilet, and don't be so loud!"

By then, every person on the tour hated our guts.

We had only fifteen minutes before Chuck dragged us out of there, and I wanted to look at the jumpsuit exhibit. My step-grandmama, Mary, got to see Elvis in concert in Nashville before he got really heavy. She said, "He was prettier than any woman I've ever laid my eyes on, and his waist was tiny."

When I saw those jumpsuits, I believed it. His little britches were so tiny. I could not hope to get my big toe into any of them. So what if at the end of his life he overate to feed his feelings? Bless his heart, I could relate. I eat emotionally too. I prefer to remember Elvis through Mary's eyes, as the most beautiful man she'd ever seen.

My favorite part of the tour was going inside Elvis's Convair 880, his private plane, which he named *Lisa Marie*. (How sad was it when she died at fifty-four? That poor family!) The plane had a big white bed in the rear. Next to the bed was a Bible. Elvis was a strong believer. I connected to that. Alongside the Bible, he had a Quran and Buddhist scripture. The tour guide said Elvis was a searcher, looking for the answer to the big question, Why me? His gift was a blessing to him, but it was also a curse he struggled with every day of his life.

I think Elvis had a raging case of impostor syndrome, fearing, *Any second now, the whole world is going to see I'm a fraud.* He searched the Bible for answers and self-medicated to deal with the demands of his life.

As a performer, you do everything you can to give everything you've got. It's not easy to show up every single night. I don't do drugs, but when I think about the pressure Elvis was under to perform—with his brutal manager, Colonel Tom Parker, working him like a mule and his personal physician, George Nichopoulos, supplying him with pills—I understand why he took them. He thought they were okay because they came from a doctor. I think Elvis was just an innocent, sweet, naïve country boy looking for love and acceptance.

Chuck shooed us out of the plane, and we went back outside to see the burial sites. Elvis, his parents, and his grandmother were all laid to rest at Graceland. The tourists around the graves were bowing their heads, full of solemnity and grace. And then we got there.

Maggie started asking a million questions:

"Is Elvis's body really in there?"

"What was he wearing when they buried him?"

"Did he have a really big coffin?"

My wild child, Tess, was spinning in circles to make herself sick. Charlie was trying to get his sisters to be quiet. Then Chuck's phone rang, and all the European tourists turned to look at him with spite in their eyes. He took the call and started talking loudly about the specs on a mobile home. He was so distracted by the conversation that he didn't realize he was standing right by Gladys Presley's stone.

The once solemn German couple next to me had been squalling over the graves. When Chuck, oblivious, came to a stop near Vernon's, waving his hand while making a sales pitch, the woman looked like she wanted to kill him.

Get in line, lady.

CHAPTER 12

My Triple Life

Everyone has a public life, the person you show the world. Think about how you act on social media, how you chat at parties, how you smile at school pickup.

Most of us also have a private life, the person you are behind closed doors with your family and close friends. It's the version of you who shares your deepest, darkest secrets, goes one wine over the line at dinner, and giggles at dirty jokes.

Some of us have a secret life, the one in your head, with all the fears, insecurities, hopes, and dreams that you'd never tell another soul or they'd think you were a lunatic.

For years, the dividing lines between my public, private, and secret lives were blurred. I always had a problem with boundaries, and talking my head off in public about my private life is sort of my thing.

MY PUBLIC LIFE

My public life in San Antonio, where we moved for Chuck's job, was a stay-at-home mom whose kids swam in the pool. We had so much to do around town, like going to children's museums. (Back in Morristown, we didn't even have a Target.) We bought passes to Six Flags Fiesta Texas. We went to SeaWorld and the Alamo. We lived like we were on a permanent vacation. We had a ball!

I love the Hispanic culture there. My step-granddaddy, Frank, one of the great loves of my life, was half Mexican and half Arapaho, and I was in heaven to be reminded of him daily. In San Antonio, you couldn't walk two blocks without running into a mariachi band. A darling preschool director told me the Hispanic women have a superstition: If they see a really cute baby, they have to touch it or something bad will happen. Tess was a yummy, beautiful toddler. You could have eaten her chunky little legs off. Whenever I took her into a store, the Hispanic women just squealed over her and squeezed and kissed her.

Chuck did well in San Antonio. They gave him an award at their annual gala, which I dubbed the Trailer Prom. All the women wore evening gowns. The men wore tuxes. Chuck's cummerbund had the Texas flag on it, and I could have died. It was kind of a joke, but he was so proud of his region. And I was proud of him for how well he was doing.

We were the very (public) picture of a happy family. A successful father and husband in his Lone Star accessories. A stay-at-home mom whose kids swam in the pool, took dance, played soccer, and were squeezed by *abuelas* at Target.

MY OTHER PUBLIC LIFE

After midnight, I wasn't just a mom and wife. I was a stand-up comedian who brought my public image as a mom and wife onstage at the Rivercenter Comedy Club. Who goes to comedy clubs at midnight? Not my demographic. I was a thirty-five-year-old mother of three. The audience was college-age kids who were high on marijuana if they weren't drunk. They were not getting up to go to work the next day or taking their children to school.

The comics who performed there were mainly male, very macho, very predictable. They *all* did impressions of Arnold Schwarzenegger and had blue material. I stood out because I was a woman who got up in capri pants and kitten heels and told a story about making Charlie play T-ball when he was five. He hated it. It was a hundred degrees and the games felt like they lasted three hours. No one ever hit a ball or threw a ball or caught a ball. For the entire season, Charlie would lie down in the outfield in a fetal position, using his glove as a pillow. Every now and again, he'd pop his head up and say, "Water!" Maggie, two, would climb down from the bleachers in her crown, wand, tutu, and pink prostitute shoes from Walmart, and run out onto the field to give her brother water. Once, she stopped halfway, pulled her panties to the side, and pooped on the field. I had to get a stick and flick it into the woods, or a child might've stepped on it or thought it was a Milk Dud. Even though the audience wanted rowdy and nasty comedy between tequila shots, I still did well, which proves that jokes about confusing poop with chocolate are funny to everyone.

I may have projected this onto myself, but as a female comedian, I worried that if I was even a little bit attractive, I might not be taken seriously. I'd read once that Phyllis Diller frizzed out her hair and wore unflattering costumes on purpose because she felt no one would pay attention to her comedy otherwise. Joan Rivers was always very self-deprecating. She looked polished, but not sexy. Female comedians talk all the time about how you can't be funny *and* pretty, and I went through a period where I felt that way. Male comedians don't have to go through that. That messed with my head. I intentionally downplayed my looks.

What I'm saying is I was no Pamela Anderson up there. I dressed like a mom onstage, in floral capris from Harold's and a kitten heel. My cleavage was kept hidden. I had a horrible bob at the time too. I didn't have to do much to look wrung out because I was so exhausted. Self-deprecation worked its way into my comedy—where it remains to this day.

Austin was an hour and thirty minutes from San Antonio, and its comedy scene was top-tier in the whole United States. I started going to the Cap City Comedy Club, one of the country's best. It was co-owned by Rich Miller, who was the brother of Dennis Miller from *Saturday Night Live* and Jimmy Miller, a Hollywood manager. I felt like this was where I was supposed to be.

Cap City had a Wednesday night show called "Chick Schtick" for female comics. I drove for ninety minutes to do a ten-minute set. The club manager/owner, Margie Coyle, had a gift for spotting talent. She liked my set and wanted me back! After just one set with me as opener, she moved me up to headliner, the first time that happened in their history.

I did that show every night for a week, getting home at 2:00 A.M. and then waking up with the kids four hours later. So, in a way, my personal life as an exhausted mom, with stories about T-ball, helped my public life as a stand-up. But my public life as a stand-up, having to perform at midnight, did not help my life as a mom.

Chuck always said, "I've got the kids. You go ahead."

Some friends came to see me perform, and they had a ball. But a lot of the other moms asked, "Are you sure you want to be doing this? You're exhausted all the time."

I didn't dare tell them that what motivated me was my secret life, the one that had lived in my head since I was five. *By doing these shows*, I thought, *I'm going to get discovered and become a star one day.*

WHEN YOUR SECRET LIFE GOES PUBLIC

Chuck was transferred again, and we relocated back to where it all began for us—Knoxville, Tennessee—to be closer to the home office. I was glad to be in the same state as my parents again, but I hated to leave San Antonio, our church there, and all my wonderful, diverse friends and neighbors.

We settled into a new (but old) public life: Chuck, the hard-working dad, and me, the stay-at-home mom. I had to find a new church and a new way to do comedy. I got a spot on a small tour called Southern Fried Chicks with two other female co-medians. That led to the Search for the Funniest Mom in America competition on Nick at Nite. I didn't win, but I was the runner-up. Always the bridesmaid, never the bride.

One day, I drove to Dick's Sporting Goods to buy a jockstrap for Charlie, who was playing middle school football. I was only vaguely aware that jock straps even existed. I didn't know what to buy. I had to ask a salesperson what to get and found out I needed a cup to go with it. Okay, as long as my baby wouldn't get hurt, I'd buy a whole tea service of cups.

My phone rang when I was in the parking lot, and I picked up.

"Is this Leanne Morgan?" a man asked.

"Yes?"

"My name is Mike Clements. I'm a producer with Warner Bros. in L.A. We think we can build a sitcom around you and your comedy."

"You *what*?"

"We think you're the next Bill Cosby."

Okay, no one likes to say that name anymore. But back then, when a showbiz producer said you were going to be the next Bill Cosby, it was a big deal.

Mike worked with Tom Werner of Carsey-Werner Productions, the same company that made *Roseanne*, *The Cosby Show*, and dozens of other long-running hits. I listened to his words, but I didn't believe what I was hearing. I mean, I didn't think the man was lying to me. He sounded sincere. But the next Bill Cosby? Me? *What in the world?*

I got the full story out of him. Unbeknownst to me, Jimmy Miller, a Hollywood manager, asked his brother Rich, owner of Cap City in Austin, whether he'd scouted out any fresh comedy talent in the middle of the country who could be developed into TV stars. Rich told Jimmy, "There's this woman from Tennessee . . ." Jimmy was intrigued, so Rich sent him my CD (just a collection of bits from a few shows). I didn't even know he'd done it. Jimmy sent my CD to Tom Werner, and that was where Mike Clements came in.

A comic once told me, "You have a better chance of winning the lottery than getting a TV show on the air." Well, that might be true . . . for that guy. I grew up watching sitcoms, and now I was going to have my own. My dream was coming true. All it took was for Hollywood to discover me. And now they'd turn me into a star overnight.

From that phone call on, things moved very quickly. They flew me out to Los Angeles to meet with writers. People were saying all kinds of flattering things, and my cheeks hurt from smiling and saying, "Why, thank you, my angel!" a hundred times a day.

Mike set up a showcase at the Laugh Factory on Sunset Boulevard for me to perform for executives at ABC, NBC, CBS, and Fox, all the big networks at the time. I was scared out of my mind to do comedy for all these network people. I put on a flattering dress and heels and curled my hair. If they were expecting the then-typical leather pants and jacket look, they were in for a surprise!

I arrived at the club with Mike and was a bit taken aback when I saw the sign out front.

"Sultans of Comedy Night?" he said. "What does that mean?"

"Sultan, like in *Aladdin*?" I asked.

Mike had no idea he'd booked my twenty-minute slot in the middle of a lineup of Middle Eastern comics on the night of their big fundraiser for their community center. Not only were all the performers Middle Eastern, but so was everyone in the audience. I was hoping they'd like to hear about how much my old-soul son loved gospel bluegrass icon Dr. Ralph Stanley. They probably didn't know the King of Mountain Soul.

I was already gripped by my usual vomit/diarrhea nerves, and now this. All the comedians looked at me with "What in the world is *she* doing here?" expressions. Who could blame them? Here I was, swooping in to do a twenty-minute set. Plus, they were trying to raise money to buy a Ping-Pong table, and I had nothing to do with that. They were real peeved, and I did not blame them.

My nerves! I really needed to run to the bathroom.

"It's going to be fine," said Mike as sweat sprouted on his forehead. He got a seat in the back and was probably praying.

The MC was named Peter the Persian. He introduced each act. Gulda the Mean Turk. Basil the Armenian. When it was my turn, he announced me by saying, "You know you're a racist when you talk with a southern accent!" He didn't put the mike back in the stand; he just flung it at me. It was not good, but I had to suck it up and act like nothing happened because all those network people were there.

"Thank you, Peter!" I said, like he'd been sweet. About five minutes into my set, he started flashing the signal that says "your time is up, get off the stage." I was supposed to get twenty minutes, so I ignored it and focused on myself.

I ran though some of my latest material, stuff that killed at Cap City, like having to prostitute myself to my husband for Stride Rites for the kids. I killed with my bit about hateful low-rise blue jeans: "Have you girls bought pants in the last five years? My goodness. I went into the Gap and this darling little nineteen-year-old heifer brought in a pair of blue jeans to try on. The zipper, honest to goodness, was two inches long. It hit me right at my doings. And I said to the salesgirl, 'Is my stomach supposed to be hanging out over my blue jeans? It looks like a small purse.' I showed her my panties riding up in the back and asked, 'Is it supposed to be hanging out this far?' She said, 'No. You're supposed to wear a thong.' And I said, 'Excuse me. I'm a Christian. I don't use my panties for evil.'"

There are times when I've bombed like nobody's business. That night, the crowd was with me. The other comedians wouldn't even speak to me, but that's okay. It was one of the best sets of my life.

Mike and I went out to celebrate after the show. He said,

"Leanne, I have figured something out. You are not a southern comedian. I know you've got a thick accent. But what you talk about is not southern. It's universal. That's why it works."

"I don't think my son listening to gospel bluegrass is universal, Mike."

"But those women hate low-rise blue jeans," he said. "They related. You are talking about what they live, and that's why they like you! They want their kids to have good shoes too!"

The whole night, I was on cloud nine. The next day, we went to every network and pitched the show to the same people who saw me kill at the Laugh Factory. ABC bought the show before we got out of the parking lot.

THE SECRET IS OUT

I had an official network deal. Papers were signed. The ink was dry. I felt like I could talk about what was happening to me, and I did. I told my family about it. I gave updates to my friends. I might've stopped strangers on the street with the news.

When the network said they wanted Paula Deen to play my mother, I was thrilled. She was at the peak of her fame, with a chain of restaurants, bestselling books, and hit TV shows on the Food Network. And this woman was going to be my costar? It was almost too much to believe.

The network flew me to New Orleans to meet her. She was doing an event at a casino. She invited me to talk to her outside while she had a cigarette and a Diet Pepsi. Paula looked exactly like herself. She was a real beauty, with Elizabeth Taylor violet eyes and perfect ash-blond hair. She was sweet and down to earth. Naturally, I was tickled to meet her.

"Leanne, tell me your story," she said.

So I did. I told her about growing up in Adams, how my

parents owned a meat processing business, how I got started in comedy by selling jewelry, and that I was married and had three babies in five years.

She said, "I believe you are who you say you are." She pointed a cigarette at me and added, "I'm too young to play your mama. But I'll do it."

I passed her test.

Once she was on board, it was on like Donkey Kong. I told everyone who'd listen about how my secret dream life was turning into reality. It was all too easy to work it into the conversation, as in:

"Hi, Leanne. How are you?"

"I'm doing great. A network is developing a show about my life! And now they want to fly me back to L.A. to meet with writers. For my sitcom. The one I'm going to star in. With Paula Deen."

It's not bragging if you're just stating the facts. Right?

They paired me with a writer from California who was a surfing-with-the-dolphins kind of gal, and I loved her. When she finished the pilot script, the next step was going to be shooting it on a soundstage with a live audience.

It was all coming together, like this sitcom was fated to happen. It felt inevitable. My secret dream was going to become my public reality, and I could not wait for it to happen.

And then, disaster.

MY PRIVATE HADES

The writers' strike of 2007 hit, and Hollywood ground to a halt. The producer called and said, "It's over. It's not happening." Scripted TV died that day for a lot of people, not just me. The strike brought on the era of *Keeping Up with the Kardashians* and other reality shows. Producers saw a way to create inexpensive programs without writers, so in a way, the strikers shot themselves in the foot. (This was all way before streaming.)

Mike called and tried to reassure me. "This happens all the time," he said. "I'm sorry."

He was so sweet, and we stayed friends. For Hollywood people, if a show falls apart on Tuesday, by Wednesday they're on to the next. It was an "oh well" moment for him.

But I thought this was going to change my life! When I learned my deal was dead, I was in shock. For nearly a year, I was told I was going to be the next Cosby, Roseanne, Seinfeld, what have you. It was boom, boom, boom, flying to L.A., flying to New Orleans, wowing execs, nonstop flattery, and then ... *crash*.

It wasn't anyone's fault. Things end suddenly in television. But I didn't know how Hollywood worked. I had no idea that even if the pilot got made, it was still unlikely the show would make it all the way to the network schedule. The ABC deal was my first rodeo. I believed everything the producers told me. Other people might have brushed off a dead deal with a cheerful, "Oh well, that's that." Not me. I was devastated. When you ride such a high, you have a long way to fall, and that was exactly what happened to me.

I took to my bed and got into a fetal position.

At the time, Chuck was traveling for work and was delayed for a day in Utah. I reached him when he was pulling into the parking lot of a sporting goods store in Ogden to buy ski pants. I told him what happened and was met with silence.

Finally, he said, "There's a man and two toddlers here with a box full of beagle puppies. I'm going to buy one."

This was his response to the news of my misery? I thought I was going to be a TV star! A puppy wasn't going to fix me.

"It's not a good time for me, Chuck," I said. "I don't have the strength to potty train a puppy." And we already had a prissy and needy toy dachshund, Puddin, who we all worshipped. If there was a Miss Tennessee for dachshunds, she would have won.

He said, "It'll be fine," and hung up. Chuck just does what he wants. He brought that puppy home on the plane.

I had to admit, the dog was stunning. He had blue eyes and a white-and-brown coat. When he ran, his ears would go straight out like he was flying. We named him Ogie, after his birthplace of Ogden, Utah. He would charge through the house and do figure eights, as cute as could be. If I so much as looked at him, he'd get so excited he'd pee on the carpet. But as precious and darling and yummy as he was, I couldn't enjoy him. I couldn't enjoy *anything*. I was looking at the world through gray glasses.

I couldn't see it at the time, but looking back, I believe the failure of that show was God's protection over me and my family. I would have had to move to Los Angeles. People told me, "Don't bring your family, though. Don't let your husband quit his job because the show might not make it. But you have to live out here in case it does."

If my prayers had been answered, I would have had to be away from my children, who were in elementary and middle school. It was a terrible time in their lives to leave them, and being apart would have killed me. But I was swept up in the fantasy and couldn't see past those stars in my eyes. I'd been trying to figure out how we could make that work, but there was no way I could've been funny in a miserable state. It would have been a disaster in every way.

Disappointment is a severely underrated emotion, I learned.

I had let my secret out, and it was thrown back in my face. I was crushed at the time. But we don't always realize in the moment how not getting what we want, when we want it, can be better in the end for us and the people we love.

But now I know the wisdom and grace of unanswered prayers.

CHAPTER 13

The BFF Breakup

Stressful things happen to everybody, like moving, getting divorced, losing a loved one, experiencing a serious injury or illness, and losing a job. By the time they reach their forties, most people have gone through a few of these. And they are not fun.

I want to add another big one to the list. For me, this experience was just as stressful as some of the others, and its terrible effects lasted a lot longer.

I'm talking about being dumped by a best friend.

WE WERE AS THICK AS THIEVES

I met Debbie when we moved back to Knoxville from San Antonio. Almost from our first encounter, she clung to me. Why? Because I was fun. Yes, *so fun*! I felt drawn to her too. We met at a party for our husbands' company when Chuck first signed on. She came up to me and was very helpful. "I'll tell you everything you need to know," she said, leaning close. I was relieved someone had offered to show me the ropes of how things worked socially in that company. She made me feel safe and protected in this new group of people, and I responded to that.

From then on, we gravitated toward each other at work functions and our kids' games. We went on double dates. Eventually, we introduced each other to our parents, and we got close to them too. Lucille adored Debbie. When Debbie's daddy died, my son, Charlie, was a pallbearer at his funeral.

We did everything together, from wacky diets to CrossFit. I talked about our hijinks in my act, as if Debbie and I were the modern-day Tennessee equivalent of Lucy and Ethel.

She was raised in a strict denomination. I was raised Methodist, which was more loosey-goosey. Methodists were kumbaya. It was all about peace and love and taking a hot dish to a friend in need. I barely read the Bible. Debbie's upbringing was sheltered, so I had to teach her about secular things, like camel toe. She invited us to go to church with her, and we started going. It was a wonderful place, just a loving environment. The pastor was a Vietnam vet with an unbelievable testimony—a funny, darling, down-to-earth, accepting, precious man. He's older now, but I hope he lives long enough to preach at my funeral. I always see him in a cute tracksuit at the grocery store.

Our kids went to the same school. Our husbands worked for the same company. Our lives were very intertwined. We were joined at the hip, together *all the time.* I look back now and realize how unhealthy that was. But at the time, I thought I'd found my very best friend.

THE GREAT GHOSTING

Just to set the scene, the Great Ghosting happened at the same time as the Great Recession.

Leading up to that, the Morgans were crushing it. For several years, we shared a second home by a lake with two families we adored. One of my favorite things was sitting on the deck, looking out at the cove, and drinking coffee. The kids were happy in private school. Chuck was a vice president at his company. I had bounced back from the sitcom disaster and was booking a lot of corporate events, parties, conventions, and fundraisers. Everyone was doing great. Not a worry in the world.

When the recession hit, my career came to a complete halt. During the economic downturn, companies cut way back on events. If they had them at all, they spent more on shrimp than entertainment.

Chuck's dad passed suddenly in 2010. The housing market had crashed. It was a scary time for everyone, including us. Some of Chuck's colleagues were fired. He was under a mountain of stress about all these changes.

I woke up one night at 2:00 and found him in the living room, using a loud saw. (FYI: If you ever find your husband in the middle of the night with a power tool in his hands, run.)

"What are you doing?" I asked.

"I'm fixing Maggie's ceiling fan."

"The kids are trying to sleep. They have school in the morning."

"Leave me alone, Leanne!" he yelled.

Oh, my God. He's losing it, I thought.

I relied on my friends to keep me sane, especially Debbie. I told her *everything* about what was going on with me, how bad it felt to beg for gigs only to get nothing, how stressed-out and grieving Chuck was—every detail, including thoughts I'd never burden my husband with.

On one of our daily walks, I opened my heart and said to her, "Things are not great at home right now. I'm worried that something scary is coming on top of all this."

She said, "Well, I have great news. We booked a ski vacation, and I'm remodeling the kitchen. You have to help me pick out tiles."

In disbelief, I listened to her go on. I'd just opened up about how we were hurting, and she changed the subject to her vacation and backsplash.

Was that rude of her, or was it wrong of me to have selfishly dumped my problems on her? Then again, she was my best friend. If she felt bad about something, I'd listen to her all day long about it. Instead of comforting me, she was rubbing her good fortune in my face when she knew we were down.

I bit my lip and kept on walking. I gave her the benefit of the doubt based on our long history as BFFs. The recession was a frightening time. We all went a bit nuts.

Putting on a smile, I asked, "So what are you doing this weekend? We could grill some steaks at our house." We hadn't had a family playdate in ages.

"Sorry, I can't," she said. "We're going on the boat with [the company's new president and his wife]. They are so sweet! I just love them. I can tell we're going to be such good friends."

That was a turning point for us. Debbie started acting weird toward me at company trips and functions and started spending more time with the company president's wife. All of a sudden, I wasn't invited to breakfasts with our friend group. I heard about their spa weekends after the fact. Debbie was the organizer, and she was excluding me. I knew it was happening, but I was naïve and thought it was an oversight.

One day, I saw Debbie in the parking lot of our gym. I went over to her car to say, "Hey, girl, hey."

She stepped out, looked at me with disgust, and said, "What do *you* want?"

"Nothing," I said, confused, hurt, taken aback. "What's going on? Are you going inside?"

She didn't answer. She flipped her hair (à la Regina George) and walked into the gym. I stood in the parking lot staring after her, completely stunned by her behavior. I had no idea what I'd done. Debbie wasn't angry per se. She was just done—or as the kids say, "done-done"—with me. From that day on, she refused to talk to me at all. Not a word.

Now, if Chuck stopped talking to me, I'd barely notice. If he stopped grabbing my boob and flaring his nostrils at me, then I'd be worried.

I tried to talk to Chuck about Debbie, but he was no help. "Let it go, Leanne," he said. "Who cares?"

He didn't understand how much it hurt to be treated like an outcast by someone I thought of as my best friend. For weeks, it wouldn't sink in that she didn't love me anymore. I still loved her. My emotions didn't turn on and off like a light switch.

Debbie and I used to talk from wake-up to bedtime, and now those hours were silent and empty. When she cut me off, it was like going cold turkey on chatting.

MEAN GIRLS, PERIMENOPAUSE STYLE

I tried to engage with the other women in our friend group by sending little heartfelt texts that said, "I don't know what in the world happened, but I miss y'all." I didn't get much back. At school functions, I overheard some of them talking about parties I hadn't been invited to. As they headed off for coffee together after drop-off, they walked right by me.

It was horrible! We were at the age when most women start perimenopause. All our hormones were going crazy, and it turned us back into adolescents with wild emotions. Were we in middle school all over again? *What in the world?* I was feeling things I'd never felt before, like jealousy and insecurity about friendships. I was up and down and freaked out. I just wanted to take to the bed.

It sounds so stupid because we were grown women with children and homes and lives that needed tending to. And yet this social split triggered intense, bonkers emotions in all of us. When friends break up, people have to choose sides, and I seemed to be on the losing end of that. Or maybe they didn't mean to avoid me. Maybe they just thought, *Leanne hasn't been around lately. She must be super busy.* And then they got on with their own busy lives.

AS OPRAH MIGHT SAY, "LET THE HEALING BEGIN!" (IT DIDN'T)

Dr. Phil once espoused, "People say, 'Time heals all wounds.' . . . Time heals nothing. It's what you do in that time."

Well, y'all, I did nothing good with my time.

I could have exercised, but that had been my thing with Debbie. Walking alone made me miss her terribly, so I stopped doing it. In a few months, I gained twenty-five pounds.

I could have prayed and strengthened my faith. Instead, I obsessed about my loneliness and replayed every moment of rejection over and over again in my mind.

I could have talked to a professional (I do love talking!) to guide me to a healthier frame of a mind. Instead, I stewed in my misery and talked about it *a lot* to people who were not trained therapists.

I could have thought harder about what my role might have been in all this. Did I do something I wasn't aware of?

My sweet mama let me beat it to death. Bless her heart, she would listen to me for hours at a time without shutting me down. Lucille doesn't do drama, so she didn't trash Debbie to make me feel better. She just said, "It'll be all right. I promise."

Beth, the protective sister, wanted to slap Debbie's teeth out. She stoked my resentment. "I cannot believe what she did!" she said. "Have you seen her vacation pictures on Facebook?"

No one was more sick and tired of this situation than I was, but I kept talking about it anyway. I had no idea what Debbie was saying to others about me and the breakup, but I felt compelled to state my case about what happened so they would know my side of it. No one gave a hoot. They were probably going through their own perimenopausal torment.

If only I'd taken a pottery class to get my mind off it! I would've felt better. I'd also have twenty matching bowls to show for it. Maybe even a nice platter.

One friend who wasn't part of this group picked me up for lunch during the peak of my defensiveness about the breakup. She came to a stop at a red light just as I was describing a tiny nuance of Debbie's behavior that had been looping in my brain since 3:00 A.M.

She said, "Leanne, you're being childish. You're acting like a kid who was left alone in the sandbox."

"That's not it," I said. It was bigger and deeper than that!

Years later, this "you're being childish" friend got ghosted by her BFF. She called me in tears and said, "Okay, now I get it."

For years after the breakup, I lurked daily on Debbie's and Team Debbie's social media pages, studying pictures of all the lunches, dinners, and parties I wasn't invited to. Maggie, then in high school, found me crying over Debbie's Facebook page one day and said, "Why would you do that? You're just sitting here, punishing yourself. It's not healthy. You should unfriend her."

To come off like a healthy person with high self-esteem in real life, I had to pretend I didn't care and wasn't hurt online. So I kept liking my ex-friends' posts about how much fun they had without me.

Social media is twisted.

Beth went through something similar herself several years ago. She, too, went to her former BFF's Instagram page a dozen times a day. Not only that, but she commented on her ex-friend's posts in a masochistic effort to win back her friendship. Lord, I never did that. I still had a tiny speck of pride.

"Beth, honey, go buy some clay and throw a pot," I said. "It'll make you feel better."

She didn't take my advice, but she's okay now. It took her forever to get over that woman, and, boy, could I relate.

HOW I FINALLY GOT OVER IT (AND YOU CAN TOO)

For a couple of years, my family lived with a big black cloud hovering over us. It wasn't just the recession and Debbie's dumping me. My father-in-law's death was very difficult. I was perimenopausal and didn't feel right. Unbeknownst to me, my thyroid had crashed. I didn't have friends to go places and do stuff with. It was a long, sad time, and I didn't cope effectively. It's a good thing I wasn't hooked on whiskey.

I'll be honest. I was mad at God. I kept asking, *Why in the world is this happening?*

Meanwhile, Chuck started going to a men's Bible study, and it changed him. Suddenly, he was all about forgiveness and serving others. I was still stuck in feeling sorry for myself.

One night, Chuck and I were sitting at the kitchen table. I was just so frustrated and worried about it all. "Is everything going to be okay?" I asked.

Chuck said, "Leanne, get a grip. Everything *is* okay."

"It's not okay!" But it really was. Through all that uncertainty, Chuck had kept us afloat. We didn't lose anything. The kids stayed in private school.

He started pacing the room. "What are we doing, Leanne?" he asked. "Why are we not helping people?"

Huh? "What are you talking about?"

"We need to help people," he said. "There are others suffering much worse than we are."

My husband had always been freehearted, volunteering and giving generously to others while somehow being very frugal. But now he was going to extremes.

Chuck came home from work and said to me, "Empty your dresser."

"What? Why?"

"A woman at work just left her terrible husband. She and her kids have no furniture, so we're going to give her some of ours."

I said, "What am I going to do with my panties?"

"You'll find somewhere to put your panties." The next thing I knew, my undies were on the bedroom floor and the dresser was loaded in the truck.

He was supposed to collect rent from some people who lived in properties he and his father owned, and if the renters didn't have the money, he'd say, "Okay." And then he'd go out and buy basketball hoops and Justin Bieber dolls for their children to make sure they had a nice Christmas. He wanted me to collect the rent instead of him because he was getting too involved with these families. But I couldn't do it either. Those people lived rent free at times because Chuck and I were too soft-hearted to evict them. Chuck also started volunteering at East Tennessee Children's Hospital to cuddle drug-dependent babies.

My husband's service to others at that low period in our lives inspired me to get involved with a charity that helps homeless women in Knoxville. Chuck went with me to hand out clothing, ChapStick, toiletries, bras, and underwear to those in need. It turns out I have a gift with homeless women. They trusted me and (you'll never guess) thought I was fun. I found Berenice a 48G bra—a victory for me—and she gave me her turtle soup recipe. I've not used that recipe yet. (Anyone know where I can buy a turtle?)

She was from Arkansas and told me, "I've got a problem with fighting."

I suggested she go to the Salvation Army to get some rest and a shower, and she said, "They won't let me in there."

"Why?"

"Because I bite."

We got along great. She never bit me.

By loving on these women, I got a good lesson about being aware of what other people were going through. I empathized with them and did what I could to make them feel better. That lifted me up and gave me a new perspective on the whole Debbie thing.

All along, I'd been asking, "Why did she do this to me?" I saw the breakup differently when I asked a new question: "What was she going through that caused her to be mean to me?"

You never really know what someone else is going through or what they're thinking. Debbie could have had all kinds of things going on, but since she wasn't telling me, anything I came up with would just be a guess at best. Since I'd never really have an explanation, I had to just let go of the idea of getting one, or being owed one, forgive, and move on.

THE GREAT FORGIVING

My road to forgiveness for Debbie—and myself—was long. It was winding. Sorry, Dr. Phil. I wallered for *years*. But eventually, I forgave myself for being obsessed with an ending that was actually a blessing in disguise. I learned to have compassion for Debbie too.

I think God removes people from your life who really don't care about you to make room for people who do. With Debbie out of my life, I was blessed to make wonderful friendships with precious, down-to-earth women who didn't know or care about my husband's career or my own. They loved me for who I am, and I'm still friends with them today.

There's another relevant quote that applies to this: "Don't worry about people God removed from your life. He heard conversations you didn't. He saw things you couldn't and made moves you wouldn't." He really did protect me by ending that friendship, even if I didn't understand it for a while.

Eventually, I became very busy in my career and didn't have time to look at Debbie's (or anyone's) Facebook page. The whole drama faded in my mind and all but disappeared. We both still lived in Knoxville, and our husbands continued to work at the same company. Chuck and I were invited to gatherings that Debbie and her husband also attended. At these parties, Debbie and I greeted each other cordially, and that was it. I don't mind seeing her. If anything, I'm sure she felt just as uncomfortable about seeing me (how the tables had flipped).

I've got a lot of flaws. I said nasty things about her in the past; I'm not perfect. But these days, when I see her, I'm kind to her. I'm fifty-eight years old. I've learned that you end up with only a few really close friends, the kind who will drop everything to come and help you, the kind who love you for who you are, not what your husband does for a living or what you can do for them.

To this day, fans ask me, "Whatever happened to that woman you did CrossFit with?"

Well, I forgave her.

She's where she's supposed to be, and so am I. And I appreciate what I learned from her about real friendship. When you're forty, feeling good and healthy, it's easy to be friends. But when you get to your fifties and sixties, things can happen. God forbid you get sick, or a spouse passes, or any number of terrible things go down. You need your real friends around you. Now I know for sure who those people are, thanks in part to Debbie.

I Love a Dog, Except for One

As you know, I am a dog person. Starting with Honey, my Peekapoo, I've kissed all my dogs on the mouth and cradled them like babies. My dachshund, Puddin, was like a child to me. I carried her around and fed her with a spoon. I bought her toys. I didn't dress her up because she had a sensory issue. But otherwise, she was like my fourth baby.

One of our beloved beagles died recently. Ogie was old and white in the face. When he got in the bed at night, Chuck pulled him up against him and spooned him. While my husband clutched him, that old beagle gave me an intense look, like, *I don't want him. I want you!* He just stared at me, imploringly. I whispered, "Hold on, hold on." As soon as Chuck fell asleep, that beagle scooched over into the crook of my legs. All babies want their mama! Every other time of the day, Ogie was Chuck Morgan's best friend.

When Puddin died, Ogie and I grieved and cried and shook. He quit eating. I was not ready for another dog. But then Maggie found Gigi online at a beagle rescue website. Two people from the rescue brought Gigi to our house. The guy looked like a member of the band Foghat, with '80s hair, a middle part and wings. He and his wife put us through the wringer to make sure Gigi would be happy with us. They stayed for hours, going through the whole house, making us swear we'd fix a hole in the fence and install a doggie door. They ran a background check on us like we were adopting a baby. Gigi was tiny—a pocket beagle—and very shy at first because she'd been abused. I thought she was cute, but I didn't think I could open my heart to another dog.

Within two days, I was madly in love with her. Now when she gets in the bed, she turns around two or three times and then backs her tiny butthole up against my face. And I don't care because she is so yummy and cute. We sit and kiss and hug all day long.

The only dog we've owned who I didn't let put her butthole against my face was a husky Chuck found tied up and neglected behind one of his rental homes. Ava was as big as a pony and had a wild look in her eyes.

Our friend who was a vet said, "This dog may have wolf in her. You cannot take her to a regular vet like me."

I didn't know she was part wolf or I never would have let her in the house. When she growled, showing a mouthful of sharp teeth, I nearly peed myself. She insisted on getting in bed and sleeping right between Chuck and me, and I feared for my life every night. Huskies needs to work and mush and stuff. I didn't have time to walk Ava several times a day or get on a dogsled. So she had a lot of nervous energy and paced in the night. When she did get out, she'd take off running and somebody would have to bring her back. I was scared she'd eat our other dogs. It was a holy nightmare.

We fostered her until somebody up north took her. It was just in time because caring for her almost killed me. I still find her hair in the microwave. It's been twelve years.

CHAPTER 14

How to Rock a Swim Dress

People say fifty is the new thirty or forty. Let's settle on fifty being the new thirty-five. It's all about how you feel, not some number.

Or maybe it is a little bit about a number. I don't want to scare anyone. It's entirely possible to be fifty and still feel in your head like you're thirty-five. But, my darling, your body doesn't care how young you feel. Your body has a mind of its own.

You might think you're still young enough to go to a rock concert. And, of course, you are. You can buy a ticket and sit in the audience. Chuck and I went to a Def Leppard and Journey concert. I thought we were going to have a fun date. When I was twenty and went to concerts, I wore crop tops and little bitty britches because I still had a metabolism and my thyroid was acting right. At this concert, everybody there was fifty or older. And they were all worried about the snack bar. I was too. People crowded around the concession stand like they were giving away gold nuggets. They acted more excited about buying big Diet Cokes and buckets of popcorn than seeing the bands.

While the concert was going on, my husband would stand up and dance a little, until he had to sit back down because of his knees. You could just tell that the guys in Journey had eaten a lot of white flour and sugar. And maybe they had done a little dope and slept with nasty women. They all looked sick and bloated, lugging around their guitars.

The lead singer of Def Leppard clearly had thyroid issues. His hair was down to his shoulders, and I swear you could see through it. He had tiny legs, a little stomach. When he hit a high note, you could see this tiny bump in his upper abdomen. I'm no doctor, but I just knew it was a hernia. I spent the rest of the concert worrying for him. I've had a hernia in the same place; it pushed through my abdominal wall. I was in so much pain I had to go to the ER. They said I needed to have surgery to put a mesh on it. And after that, it took six months to recover. The Def Leppard singer probably didn't have time to get a mesh because he was on a rock tour, bless his heart.

The concert finally ended. I used to be sad when the lights came up. At this concert, we all limped out of the arena because we had plantar fasciitis. It was like an episode of *Survivor*, with all of us climbing over trees and wading through swamps to try to get to our cars. Everyone was exhausted and desperate, saying, "We gotta get home! What are we doing here?" It was 10:00 P.M.

So, no, I'm not going to rock concerts anymore. Unless there's seating.

Here are some of the other Never Agains on my list:

SHOPPING AT VICTORIA'S SECRET

At thirty-five, I still felt twenty-five and wanted to wear the low-rise jeans that were popular at the time. And that actually worked, as long as I didn't look at my rear in the mirror. Low-rise britches required low-rise thongs. I could not do it. I felt like I was being strangled. So I just wore big panties that puffed out over the top. I was glad when that trend was over.

At forty, I kept wearing Victoria's Secret because I still had hope. Around forty-five, my body changed and expanded, but my panties stayed the same size. Before long, they were cutting me in two. That was when hope was lost, and I started buying big, comfortable flesh-toned panties and a high-rise jean.

DOING CROSSFIT

I started doing CrossFit at a gym in Knoxville with Debbie when we were in our midforties, right before perimenopause set in. At the time, CrossFit was brand-new, all the rage. The twenty-five-year-olds who taught us had fannies that looked like baseballs. I wanted my fanny to look like baseballs too.

They had us do extremely difficult military push-ups and pull-ups and flip tractor tires across a parking lot. I was enthralled by the experience even though I was scared whenever I was jerking a thirty-pound kettle ball over my head or climbing a rope twenty feet in the air. The instructors did some heavy eye-rolling as we did sloppy burpees, but they loved us because we could afford the gym membership.

It made me feel like a bad mama jama. I also really enjoyed getting up into the trainers' personal business because they were young and cute and had tons of dating drama that was fascinating to old, married me. Their love triangles and messy breakups made me flash back to my Erica Kane years, not missing them one bit.

I hoped the intense workouts would give me a new lease on life. But when my hair started to fall out from total body rebellion due to high cortisol levels and low thyroid, I decided to break that lease.

DOING PALEO

The only time I dieted to lose weight as a kid was when I was fifteen and I competed in the Fairest of the Fair pageant, the one where I ate only a can of tuna a day and nearly collapsed in my convertible on the parade route. I stopped dieting for good (almost) and stayed fit playing sports.

Mama and Beth were always on some yo-yo fad diet. One week, they ate three eggs for breakfast, three bananas for lunch, and three hot dogs for dinner. They were so weak by the end of it, they couldn't make a fist. The only time I joined in was when I took Dexatrim for a few days when I was seventeen. Dexatrim, if you don't know, was speed. We took speed as a family. We took it, and our heads would itch. And then we'd fight in the yard. So I stopped doing that.

I thought dieting was just stupid until my thirties, when my butt went from a cute bubble to a beach ball and I decided cutting back on sweets would be a good idea. And yet, somehow, I could not keep it up. I'm a cake and cookie girl.

Our CrossFit instructors asked us if we wanted to enter a contest called the Paleo Challenge to see whose bodies changed the most. For ten weeks, I ate just meat, vegetables, and fruits—no dairy, sugar, or grains. I took it very seriously, but I don't know why. I'd never stuck with a diet before in my life.

On "before" picture day, I wore spandex workout pants and a

horrible, dingy, no-support white sports bra that made me look like I had one boob. No spray tan. I didn't want to take my top off in front of the young male instructors. They didn't need to see what happened to a woman's body after she raised three kids. They'd never want to be married and have children. So Debbie and I went into the locker room to take each other's picture. She posed and pulled her stomach in, and I thought, *That's just stupid.* "Debbie, do you not want to win this thing? Because I want to win it," I said.

I had enough sense to know if you wanted to win, you had to look your worst in the "before" picture so that in the "after" picture you'd be so much cuter. When Debbie took my picture, I pulled my stomach bulge over the spandex waistband of my pants. I slumped my shoulders forward. I had a terrible look on my face.

I had no idea they were going to put those pictures on the internet. Thank God they cut my head off. When I saw it, I thought, *You really are what you eat.* I looked like a swollen white blob of hamburger bun.

The challenge was to follow the paleo diet and do CrossFit for ten weeks, and it almost killed me. But it worked. I leaned out and my body changed. I looked like a different person. Chuck and I went to Maui on a company trip during that time, and my pants were hanging off me. Nothing fit.

I made sure I had a spray tan and wore a nice sports bra for the "after" picture. I held my stomach in until my core cramped. Well, guess what? I won that competition and got three months of free torture. I mean, *training.*

Was it worth it? I lost fifteen pounds, and the very second I went off the diet and had a biscuit, I gained back what I lost, plus another ten pounds. The whole time I felt terrible! I had extreme fatigue, I couldn't poop, my breasts were super tender, and my hair was falling out. I'd doze off in the middle of the day. I could not keep my eyes open. And then at night I couldn't sleep.

As fit as the CrossFit instructors were, they didn't know much about middle-aged female bodies, hormones, and stress. The intense exercise combined with the carb deprivation was such a shock to my system that I believe it threw me into a health crisis.

So, no, turning into a miserable zombie was not worth losing fifteen pounds.

My paleo adventure was not my last diet, unfortunately. After that, whenever I went up a dress size, I tried a new diet. My fallback was always Weight Watchers. Oprah had bought a stake in the company by then, and I saw her on a commercial twirling pasta and running through tall grass. I thought, *If she can do it, I can, too!* and I signed up *again*.

Back to weekly weigh-ins, counting food points, and eating tiny portions. I was so hateful on Weight Watchers. I was in a constant bad mood, snapping at everyone, lines deepening on my forehead. I couldn't keep track of my points. Chuck wasn't even on it, and he wanted me to keep track of *his* points too. I didn't have the patience for that. And yet I kept going back. I can't tell you how many times I've downloaded that app. I do believe that Weight Watchers works. But you actually have to do it. You know what, I may try Weight Watchers again, now that we're talking about it!

LETTING SOMEONE TELL ME THE SKY ISN'T BLUE

After that paleo challenge, I was tan and thin, and people told me I looked great. But I knew something was seriously wrong with me. I was exhausted and constipated. My shower drain always had a disturbing amount of hair in it. I went to my doctor and asked him, "Do I have cancer?"

"No, you don't," he said. "You'll be fine."

A poster on his wall described low-thyroid symptoms and listed pretty much every problem I was having. I asked, "Could it be my thyroid?"

He shook his head. "We ran a thyroid panel, and you're fine."

"But look at that poster," I said. "I can't poop and my hair is falling out . . ."

"It's not your thyroid," he said, annoyed. "You're just depressed."

He wasn't listening to me. "I am depressed because I have no energy and my hair's falling out!" It was frustrating to be told my physical symptoms were all in my head when I had so many of them.

But I was taught that doctors were very smart, that they went to medical school for a hundred years, and that they knew what they were talking about. He gave me some antibiotics for a sinus infection, and I tried to be optimistic that I'd feel better soon.

But I didn't. One afternoon, I dragged myself and the kids to their orthodontist appointment and had to lean on the front desk for support. I told the receptionist, "I'm just so tired, and my doctor keeps saying there're nothing wrong with me."

She said, "There's a nurse practitioner I've been hearing wonderful things about who's really helping women. Her name is Karen Nickell. She's very much in demand with a long waiting list. It's nearly impossible to get in to see her."

As it turned out, Karen worked for a doctor who lived right next door to us. His sweet wife got me in with her!

Karen took one look at me and said, "I'm going to test you for low thyroid."

"My doctor says I'm okay," I said.

"He was probably doing an antiquated panel."

That turned out to be true. According to Karen's updated panel, my thyroid was out of whack *and* I was in adrenal fatigue. Thank God someone pointed me to someone who listened and knew what she was doing.

I still have the utmost respect for doctors. That one man who told me the sky was green when I knew it was blue was probably just overworked and pressed for time.

Karen Nickell got me back on track with thyroid medication and supplements. Even then, it still took a while to feel normal. I don't know how people go through it without a nurse practitioner in their corner. I have since realized that smart female nurse practitioners are like sleuths. They can look at the whole picture, connect the dots, and solve the mystery. They listen!

UNDERESTIMATING HORMONES

When I was young and my hormones were flowing, I had no idea that in my midforties, they'd start slowing down and cause utter havoc in my body. I always had an IUD, so my cycle wasn't an indicator. I'd never even heard the word "perimenopause" until my nurse practitioner told me, "You're soaking in it right now."

Perimenopause, in case you don't know, is a holy nightmare. I got hot flashes and would bead up with sweat at night. It never got so bad that I had to change my nightgown, but I did have to towel off at two in the morning and go back to bed. I had crazy mood shifts, going from laughing hysterically to crying hysterically. My whole family thought I was losing it. (Having two daughters with PMS while I was in perimenopause was a joy a minute for my husband and son.)

A year or two before my perimenopause symptoms showed up, my sister was dealing with her own and went to her doctor. He said, "I don't know what to tell you. Your mother went through it. You'll have to go through it too." He didn't put her on hormone replacement or even talk to her about it. His prescription was to just suffer through it. I told her, "Get a second opinion!"

Here's mine: Why suffer if you don't have to?

Karen put me on an herbal supplement called saw palmetto (*Serenoa repens*), and eventually I started taking estradiol, a bioidentical compounded hormone-balance cream—just like Suzanne Somers, queen of the ThighMaster. Because of her bioidentical hormones, Suzanne Somers looked like a movie star and actually wanted to do vulgar things with her husband until she died. I grieved over her death. I loved her!

For a few years, the proper dosing of my meds was trial and error. I was a sweaty, sleep-deprived lunatic. Karen adjusted the medication to see what combination of hormones had the best results. Now I take bioidentical estrogen, an oral progesterone, and just a tiny bit of testosterone cream. They come in a pen-like delivery system. What's best for me is one click at night and two clicks in the morning.

I live in fear that when I'm on the road, I'm going to forget my clicker. Chuck does too because then I would try to tell him about my symptoms.

"Chuck, I'm sweaty. My bladder's leaking. I have an odor!"

"Leanne, don't tell me that. Let me keep you on a pedestal."

He couldn't take it. And this from the man who saw my Cornish hen uterus on my chest.

GETTING PREGNANT

I'd always been able to get pregnant on a moment's notice. My period was like clockwork, and I knew exactly when I was ovulating. When Charlie was just over a year, I thought he needed a little brother or sister. I could tell I was ovulating and said to Chuck, "I'm ready. Let's make a baby. Meet me in the closet." I got pregnant that night.

When I turned fifty, Karen said it was time to take out my IUD. I'd had it in there for a while. "I doubt you're still ovulating," she said.

Just to be sure, she tested me, and it turned out I was very much ovulating and was still as fertile as the Napa Valley. "I can't take out that IUD! You'll have another baby!" she said.

For some crazy reason, that thrilled me. I had never been so proud of myself. You know when you see a football player get a touchdown and he does a muscle-man pose, like Tarzan, in the end zone? That was how I felt about being fertile at fifty. It was a great big, "YESSSS! I RULE!"

When I told Chuck, he turned white as a sheet. He didn't flare his nostrils at me for a month. I didn't want to have a baby at fifty either! We both had plantar fasciitis and couldn't walk across the floor in the morning. How would we run to pick up a crying baby? Tess was in high school, and her having a baby sibling didn't seem right. Lord, that baby would probably grow up to rob banks and end up in prison by twenty-one because I was too tired to parent.

I left in my IUD for another year and retested at fifty-one. Still ovulating (secret cheer to my ovaries!). We tested again at fifty-two and fifty-three. I didn't take out that IUD until my ovaries were done at fifty-four years old.

I don't mean to sound arrogant about it. I had nothing to do with my being a Fertile Myrtle. I come from farming people and was born with a strong constitution. We've got thick ankles to work in the field and lively ovaries to make dozens of Future Farmers of America. If not for all the carbs, cigarettes, and Diet Cokes I had in the '80s, there's no telling how strong my body would be today. I regret that. I might still be ovulating like Janet Jackson.

WORRYING ABOUT MY BUTT

I'd always had a booty. (Today that's in fashion, but it wasn't in the '80s when I was growing up.) But I always felt good that at least my stomach was flat. Now I have this mushy stomach too. It's like a roll of uncooked dough that sits on top of my C-section scar and under my belly button. It's known by the charming term "menopause apron." I like a high-rise jean I can stuff it into.

Nowadays, I wear cotton panties that are so big you could use them to fight a bull. Have you seen the movie *Braveheart*? You remember that big old catapult they used? They would put a boulder in a sling and send it flying to kill a bunch of women and children. That's what my panties look like. My bras are like two catapult slings sewn together. Speaking of that . . .

OBSESSING ABOUT MY BREASTS

When I got implants at thirty-three, I looked good naked and in clothes, and my confidence came back. I have no qualms about anyone getting implants in her thirties like I did.

Just be warned: When you get to your fifties, they get heavy. They weigh on you. I can't find tops that fit over my huge breasts. Buttons gape. My back hurts because I'm carrying around these extra pounds. I worry about Breast Implant Illness, which I've learned is a real thing. (No one believed in it when I got my implants, but it's been a while, and the research is in.) The symptoms are scary: chronic fatigue, headaches, joint and muscle pain, hair loss, skin rashes, dry mouth, dry eyes, brain fog, depression, anxiety, insomnia. Turns out having two foreign objects living inside your body might lead to an autoimmune condition. The good Lord thankfully spared me from that fate.

But they just don't look good anymore. They're like two bowling balls. I like to call them mamaw breasts. I look like a big old woman from pioneer times, plowing the field, cooking over a woodstove, boobs overflowing with milk to feed the family in hard times. I just recently learned that breast implants have an expiration date, and mine are past theirs. It's time for them to come out. We had a good run. But having buckets on my chest isn't a good look on me.

I'd go today and drain those things. But I bet Chuck Morgan would grieve his heart out.

READING WITHOUT GLASSES

My little daddy gave me perfect vision. I never needed glasses and didn't think I'd ever have to wear them. When I was in my midforties, I lay down to take a nap, woke up, and couldn't see. I tried to read, but the letters were all a blur. I got cute animal-print readers at T.J.Maxx, and that worked for a while. I went to my little eye doctor, who was precious, in his eighties, and looked like Mr. Magoo. He told me I had to get progressives. I hated wearing them and wanted to try contacts. That yummy little elderly man straddled me for over an hour, trying to get them in. He could not do it. I kept closing my eyes and thought, *Should we get married?*

Maggie had to put my contacts in for me because I was so grossed out at the thought of touching my own eyeball. It took me two years to figure out how to do it without gagging. I didn't ask Chuck for help because if he touched my eyeball, he might want to touch something else.

THINKING CLEARLY

Worst of all, I feel like I'm losing about ten IQ points a year. I'm in constant menopausal brain fog. I find myself walking into a room and saying, "What am I doing here?" I go to clean out a closet and end up in the driveway. I often wonder whether something is really wrong with me, like early-onset Alzheimer's. But my nurse practitioner says, "Everyone walks around this way." Many times, I've been onstage and said, "What am I talking about?" And members of the audience have had to yell out, "Beagles!" and "Def Leppard!" to get me back on track.

TAKING MY HEALTH FOR GRANTED

Recently, I went out with Maggie to a Mexican restaurant and had a spicy chicken burrito. I wound up in the doctor's office, vomiting and pooping blood. It was frightening. I came out of all that looking picked as a jaybird (southern for "frazzled"). I was pale and my hair was a mess with my roots showing. My little hairdresser squeezed me in, and I got a spray tan ASAP so I wouldn't look like a walking corpse onstage. That, plus some fake lashes, and I felt so much better. I was told the cause was some mysterious gastrointestinal problem that, heaven forbid, might come back in the future. You know what I think it was? It was God waking me up to tell me to drink more water, cut back on gluten, eat krauts, and work on my microbiome. He speaks to us all in different ways. This time, he spoke to me through my butthole.

Message received, Lord. I no longer take my health for granted. And I'm constantly taken aback by body changes.

I smell like old hay that a horse peed on.

I've got a leaky bladder and skin tags that pop up like mushrooms.

I think I've got a hiatal hernia too.

I choke on everything now. I always order ranch dressing, and people think it's because I'm a redneck. No, it's because when vinaigrette hits the back of my throat, I start coughing.

Recently, I lost my voice, just woke up and couldn't talk. By now, you know that for me, that is a fate worse than death. I had to write everything on a notepad, like, "Laryngitis sucks!" and "Feed the dogs" and "I'm constipated!" (unrelated to my laryngitis). Chuck bought a box of prunes, set it down next to me, and walked away.

I went to a specialist in Nashville who works with all the country music singers. She numbed my tongue and mouth and put this tiny flashlight down the back of my throat. "Your larynx is inflamed because of acid reflux," she said. I had no idea I had acid reflux. I just thought I shouldn't have pizza (my Weight Watchers red-flag food) late at night.

"In the meantime, you need to rest your voice until the inflammation goes down," she said. That day, I had five meetings and a sold-out show to do. I croaked out, "Would tea with honey do the trick?" It didn't.

Me not talking? Suddenly, Chuck became the needy one, staring at me, wondering what I was thinking.

WEARING A BIKINI

Back in the day, when "perimenopause" was a word I'd never heard of, I didn't know how good I had it as a size ten with a decent metabolism. And I still thought I was fat. Mama used to tell me, "You need to enjoy where you are now because you're going to look back and say, 'Wow, that was nice.'" Now I'd give anything to be that size. Why wasn't I thrilled with my shape when I had it? Imagine the condition I'll be in in my seventies! I hope that instead of pining for the body I have now that I'll still be able to walk around the block.

I've been trying to make small changes to move more, handle stress better, and eat to heal. I went on a health retreat, and they said, "You are eating food that's either killing you or healing you." I'm not perfect 100 percent of the time, but I'm trying. And I think I'm pretty cute for my age. I won't wear a bikini again, but fear of looking heavy is not going to keep me from living. Now I rock a super cute swim dress. When I get a spray tan, put on diamond stud earrings and false eyelashes, and have on a nice wedge at the pool, I feel good. I think I look like a movie star (sometimes).

Getting in shape is no longer about looking cute in my pants or impressing anyone at my class reunion. Thank God that after a certain age, no one cares what anyone looks like anyway. I just had my fortieth high school reunion. We were all just glad to be alive and not in jail. I was the only one in high heels. Everyone else had on an orthotic. They were the smart ones.

I can't worry about impressing anyone. My goals now are to be active with my grandchildren, to have the stamina to do a big comedy tour, and to stay that way for many years to come.

Ideally, we all want to live long and die quick. In the meantime, it helps to remember that everything is fleeting. Beauty fades, money comes and goes, boobs drop, stomachs get mushy, skin tags appear on your neck and armpits. You can't put your identity and your self-worth in looking young. I believe that self-worth comes from being a child of God, which nobody can take away from you. I'm pretty sure that precious Mother Teresa did not wear a bikini either.

The Empty Nest

Some parents cheer when their kids go off to college and the nest is empty. I didn't feel "woo!" about it at all.

First Charlie left. It was hard on me for him to go, but I still had Maggie and Tess at home. Nonetheless, I grieved and took to the bed and looked forward to him coming home for Thanksgiving.

The summer after his freshman year, he came home all right, and he brought his new girlfriend, Mary, with him. When he introduced us, I was very polite. Later, Charlie was alone with me in the kitchen and said, "Mom, you've got a terrible look on your forehead. You don't like Mary?"

"Nothing against her. She seems very sweet and super smart," I said. "It's just that I'm jealous because I thought you would only love me." I know it is twisted, but Charlie was my boy.

When they got engaged at twenty-two, I felt jealous and sad. I thought, *He'll go off with his wife and her people.* I'd always heard the adage that "a daughter is a daughter for life, and a son is a son until he takes a wife."

Right before their wedding, Charlie said, "Mom, you understand that Mary is going to be my immediate family, and now you're my extended family. That's biblical."

All my worries were confirmed! Why did I ever show him the Bible?

Over time, Charlie forgave me for my forehead looks. He still called and visited all the time. And let me say now how much I love my Mary. She's like another daughter to me. She's given me two precious, beautiful grandsons who are blessings from heaven. Charlie is *supposed* to cling to his wife. He's a wonderful husband and daddy, and that's what he's supposed to be doing. When I'm old in a nursing home, my girls will come by to pluck my chin hairs.

When my middle baby, Maggie, left home, it was bittersweet. Maggie is a beauty. She is smart, a good student, athletic. But we had to walk on eggshells when she was sixteen. We were all scared to death of her. She wouldn't let us eat cereal in our own home because she couldn't stand to hear us chew. Every morning, we didn't know who was coming down the stairs.

Maggie's last summer before college was the worst. She complained about how I sipped my coffee. The very breath out of my nostrils made her angry. In all fairness, she had a lot on her. She had to empty the dishwasher.

I think God knows parents grieve about their kids leaving home. We take to the bed and clutch our chests, just imagining how much we'll miss them. So God makes it easier for us by making them mean snakes so it's easier to let them go. Maggie didn't venture far for college anyway. She went twenty miles down the road to UT and came home every few weeks to take a long bath. She loves a bath, and we were thrilled whenever she showed up.

When Tess left, I missed her terribly and took to the bed, eating chocolate-covered blueberries and watching *Scandal* on Netflix. The sex scenes between Olivia and the president fascinated me. Tony Goldwyn as the president was super cute. It looked like he and Kerry Washington had intense sexual chemistry. I was convinced they were really doing it. But watching *Scandal* and ordering Jimmy John's from my bed was not living my best life. It was only a temporary distraction from the empty house.

I was proud my babies were off and doing well, but they left me alone with their daddy, and he doesn't chat. Chuck and I would just stare out into space. We were very sad. Meals were so painfully quiet that I was disgusted by the sound of my own chewing.

Were the next thirty years of my life going to be fighting with Chuck over the bedroom thermostat and begging my kids to call me or come home?

That was my fear. But as it turned out, when the kids left me, I came into my own.

CHAPTER 15

Expect It When You
Least Expect It

After going through decades of life, you reach a point where you think you know what's going to happen next. You've seen a lot and learned a lot about how the world works. You've had your highs and lows, woo-hooed in triumph and taken to the bed in sadness. But those highs and lows start to level off. You start wondering whether you have felt everything you are ever going to feel and done everything you are ever going to do.

This "stuck" mindset comes for all of us. I was deep in it after my kids left me alone with their father to stare at the walls. It was not fun. It felt like I was revving my engine, but I wasn't getting anywhere, especially in my career.

I did my best to get booked at comedy clubs, but that well was dry. Karen Mills, the comedian who opens for me on tour now, and I first started performing together in the Southern Fried Chicks tour in 2004. During my slow years, she kept me going, hustling up gigs for the two of us—corporate fundraisers, that sort of thing. I referred her for gigs too. We tried to drum up some excitement about our new tours called Hen

Party and Country Cool. But as hard as we tried, we couldn't get anything off the ground. She was my comedy lifeline, the only one who truly understood what I was going through. Karen became one of my best friends for life and is like part of the family.

I'd come to expect rejection, and that was what I got. Always the bridesmaid!

Don't feel sorry for me, though. I was doing plenty of that for myself.

ONE STEP FORWARD

My manager at the time called me and said, "There's a new online platform called Dry Bar Comedy out of Salt Lake City, and they want you to do a comedy special. Hardly anyone is going to see it live, but they'll post clips of it on their website, and at least that could lead to other things. Just do old material that's never been filmed."

Oh, Lord. Easy for him to say. My memory was fading. *Can I even remember this stuff?* I wondered, in a bit of a panic.

I'd never heard of Dry Bar, but the only other job I had that week was performing at a chamber of commerce luncheon in Dubuque, Iowa. That was how well my career was going.

Dubuque was close enough to Salt Lake City, so it made sense to pop over there to do this special. I hoped it wouldn't turn out to be the only one I ever taped. My dream was Netflix, HBO, or Amazon Prime. But that seemed like a pipe dream at that point.

Dry Bar sent me a list of words I couldn't say. They wanted a "clean" show. But what did that mean? Church clean? Family picnic clean? Definitely not jewelry party clean. Those events were R-rated, with all that urine and nipple talk.

I flew out to Salt Lake City with a spray tan. They put me in this horrible hotel that looked like you could be murdered in it. I took a shower and half my spray tan washed off my chest. *What in the world?* That had never happened before. I was suddenly ombré, and there wasn't anything I could do about it. I always felt thinner and cuter with a spray tan. Now what was I going to do?

For the filming, I wore a pair of Loft jeans with a cuff that completely cut my leg off, a flowy top, and wedges. Not a good choice!

My set was not tight because I was so rusty. The whole time, I worried about what I was saying and whether it would be flagged as inappropriate. I hadn't done this material in years, and I was stumbling over my words, trying to remember. I felt like my performance was terrible.

The Dry Bar people must have liked it, though. They posted a bunch of clips on their platform—and some of them got millions of views. Millions! I'd never seen numbers like that on any of the things I'd posted on Facebook.

Was that a sign of forward movement in my career?

I didn't know. I wasn't going backward, at least.

TWO STEPS BACK

I have always said, "I don't care what anyone thinks of me." But then I started reading the comments online about my Dry Bar clips. Most of them were very sweet. But some people wrote things that put me on the floor in a fetal position:

"You're not funny."

"Your accent is fake."

"I would rather have a puncture wound to my abdomen than listen to you."

You can't please everybody all the time, but there seemed to be a multitude of people out there who were offended by my very existence.

At first, it killed me.

One of the clips was my bit about how teenage Maggie was so offended by the sound of my chewing. People started saying I was making fun of my daughter for having misophonia, a sensory disorder I'd never heard of. One woman wrote, "Instead of mocking your child, you should get her help."

That devastated me. I would never make fun of anyone with a disorder—sensory, physical, emotional, or otherwise. My mind just does not go there. Maggie didn't have a disorder. She was just sixteen and on her period.

I found myself commenting back or messaging people privately, saying, "I would never make fun of any child. And I would never make fun of my own child if she had a disorder. I mean, good Lord, who do y'all think I am? I would not do that." I became obsessed with making those people like me. I lost hours sending messages to strangers.

I drove to Chattanooga, where Maggie was living at the time, and told her what was going on. She deserved to know. I asked, "Do you want me to tell Dry Bar to take down that clip?" We were sitting on her bed, and just being near her made me feel so much better.

"No, Mom. It's funny. Most people get it." After a pause, she said, "Let's read some of these comments like they do on Jimmy Fallon. Let's take your power back."

We looked at some clips of celebrities like Emma Stone and Paul Rudd reading "mean tweets" about them. It made me feel so much better about my own situation to see that this was an issue for pretty much everyone who put themselves out there. "Okay, let's do it," I said. Maggie and I made a video of the two of us reading some of the cruel comments, with a heavy accent, and we got so tickled. We laughed until we were weak, and that made it all right.

But the experience still set me back a bit. If you set out not wanting to offend anyone, you can't win. Logically, I knew that, but I started second-guessing everything I said, onstage and off. The fear of offending people got so bad that, for the first time in my life, I became tongue-tied.

Because of the Dry Bar special, I got a new label as a "clean comic," which guaranteed that most clubs would not book me. It did lead to my doing a handful of women's nights at sweet churches. They would have a taco truck out front and somebody selling Mary Kay in the lobby. The church girls went nuts for my act. I'm a church girl too. Clearly, they needed to go out more and have fun. Any time you get a bunch of women together fellowshipping, it's a good time. I didn't even need to say something for them to have a ball. They'd throw their ergonomic crossbody bags in the air.

Much as I enjoyed the people I met at church gigs and corporate events, the fee barely covered my travel expenses to get there, and it wasn't the kind of work I wanted to be doing. I got booked at some comedy clubs, but I couldn't sell tickets. It was just a grind. And I was nervous that some of the content in my act would bring on a new wave of mean comments. I was booked to perform for a Christian organization in Pigeon Forge and hesitated to include one of my funniest bits about Tess's gymnastics uniform when she was eleven. It was a tiny skirt and crop top that I called a "whore outfit."

I asked the pastor, Phil, a precious little man with a black pompadour hairdo, "Pastor Phil, I say 'whore' in my act. Is that okay?"

He grabbed my hands and said, "Honey, 'whore' is in the Bible. So that's okay."

I could have kissed him on the mouth. I could have squeezed him in two.

Of course, Facebook flagged the post, saying "whore outfit" was hate speech. No, it was just a funny phrase. I wasn't hating on whores. I care about whores!

COMPLETELY STALLED

A few months after the Dry Bar special, I remember going out to eat with Chuck and crying, right there in the restaurant, into my disappointing protein-and-vegetable plate. If I didn't have a full nest of children and I didn't have a career in comedy, what did I have?

He said, "Good Lord, Leanne. You're fine. Quit crying."

He's always been so empathetic.

I took a bite of broccoli. "Maybe I could open a shop in Knoxville, like a mercantile or hardware store. I'd have a big cheese wheel on the counter. We could sit around, eat cheese. Everyone would visit, like a gathering place."

Chuck said, "That's crazy."

"It could work, though!" I said.

Every day, I obsessed about what to do next.

Maybe I should bow out of comedy. Just end it. I've had a good run. It's been fun.

I can go work at Target, in bedding.

When Charlie and Mary have a baby, I'll just be a meemaw. I'll start wearing housedresses and cooking pinto beans, and that will be my life.

I prayed about it. I asked, *God, what am I supposed to do? Is comedy what I'm supposed to be doing? Should I quit? I want whatever is Your will.*

I waited for Him to show me the door out, but He never did. There was always some job to do—a private party in Knoxville, a charity fundraiser, a radio spot on SiriusXM. I always had something that kept me in the game. A huge defining moment was when Matt Williams, the creator of *Roseanne* and *Home Improvement*, saw a tape of mine and wanted to develop a sitcom around my life. It went to Nick at Nite and TV Land and, for whatever Hollywood reason, didn't make it. That was my second rodeo. And it was just as disappointing as the first.

But it felt like God was giving me these morsels as a way of saying, *Just hold on, Leanne.* If I was okay in God's eyes, then I didn't need to be worried about anyone else. I could keep doing my thing for the people who loved it and take my joy from that.

ONE LAST PUSH

For decades, I had heard from other comics that you have to put some money into your publicity and marketing to make a name for yourself. I'd never done that. I didn't even have a website. In twenty-some years, I had only three headshots made. Instead, I'd put all my earnings into the kids' uniforms and homecoming dresses. But now they were all taken care of. I had no excuse not to spend a little to invest in my career.

It didn't make sense to quit comedy without giving it one last shot. A little money was coming in from the Dry Bar special. If I used that to invest in some marketing and that didn't change things, then I would find something else to do. At that point, all my social media posts were pictures of Puddin, my dachshund. Other comics like Jim Gaffigan were smarter about it. But I knew I needed help.

I got a recommendation from an agent and hired two brothers in Plano, Texas, who had a social media marketing firm called Honest Fox Media. They had me search my house for every videotape, cassette, and photo of me doing my act, going back twenty years, and send it to them. The Texas boys edited the better-quality video clips and gave them new titles, new graphics, and new music. Their plan was to start posting the revamped clips on my social media pages on October 14, 2019. I had about 30,000 followers on all my platforms combined.

Coincidentally, the new clips would drop on the same date that Chuck and I were helping Tess move into an apartment in Brooklyn. We were so busy dealing with packing and travel that my social media relaunch all but slipped my mind.

GIANT LEAP FORWARD

We made it to New York City for Tess's move. Before we left the hotel, I checked my Facebook page. The Texas boys had posted two videos. One clip was called "When You Go to Concerts with Old People." It was about going to that Def Leppard and Journey concert with Chuck. I did that bit only once, at a theater in Chattanooga. Every time I refreshed my Facebook page, the number of views jumped. It went from a few dozen to a few hundred to many thousand.

A strange sensation rippled through my body, like a wave of energy. I know that sounds witchy. I didn't understand it, but I couldn't deny it.

I said, "Y'all, I just got the weirdest feeling that something's happening."

Chuck said, "The Uber will be here in two minutes. If we all carry three suitcases, we can get downstairs in one trip."

"I can't carry three suitcases at the same time," said Tess.

They weren't listening to me. "Y'all, *something's happening*," I said.

"What's happening is that we're leaving. Now," said Chuck.

We managed to get all of Tess's stuff into an Uber Black with a big trunk and drove across the Brooklyn Bridge to where her apartment was located. The whole ride, I rode those waves of energy as they passed through me.

A text came in from one of the Texas boys that read, "One of your clips is going crazy." I checked again, and the numbers were zooming up.

We arrived at Tess's apartment and got her settled in. I didn't look at my phone for a couple of hours, but when I checked again, that clip had been viewed by hundreds of thousands and shared many thousands of times. My social media follower count had ballooned from 30,000 to 125,000.

I texted the Texas boys, "Have you seen anything like this before?"

They wrote back, "Absolutely not. This is wild."

The revamped Def Leppard clip was the breakout moment that I never planned for or ever saw coming. People who liked it searched for other clips of mine, and the views skyrocketed all over the place. The Texas boys kept feeding new clips to my social media pages. By the end of that week, I had 500,000 followers.

By November, those club owners who refused to book me for years were calling up to say, "We want her." Women had been calling those clubs and asking about me. I started selling out everywhere, in minutes.

It was crazy. All of a sudden, I was so busy I didn't have time to cash my checks. Chuck found a dozen of them in my backpack one day and said, "Are you a drug dealer?" (Note to my husband: Drug dealers don't take checks.)

The moment it all became real to me was when Brian Dorfman (remember him from Zanies in Nashville?) and Mike Smardak from Outback Concerts, one of the biggest comedy concert promoters in the country, offered me a fifty-city tour of theaters all over the United States.

"How much does something like that pay?" I asked.

Brian said, "You'll make [a shockingly large amount] per show."

I needed a minute to lift my jaw off the floor before I could say, "*What in the world?!*" and "Yes!" Finally I was making it! And I got to buy all the Target bedding I wanted.

They put my tour dates up for sale, and so many of them sold out that Outback added another fifty cities. So it turned into a one-hundred-city tour. It felt like I'd won the lottery. I was thrilled, but I had doubts too. I asked myself, *Can I do this? Am I good enough?* At fifty-five, I learned you're never too old for impostor syndrome. Now that people had high expectations of me, could I live up to them?

I pushed down all that unhelpful doubt and just forged ahead, reminding myself that this was what I'd prayed for. I asked God to show me a door, and it opened into the career I'd dreamed about since I was five.

The timing could not have been happenstance. Literally the same day I got my last child settled in her adult life, my career exploded.

In my head, I'd almost settled into the idea that nothing new was going to happen in my life, and that was when everything changed.

I'm not telling you this story to brag about how I became an overnight success after twenty-two years in comedy. I hold it up to you as proof that patience and faith can work wonders. There is no doubt in my mind that God chose the moment for me. He waited until my babies were grown before I came into my own.

But it never would have happened if I hadn't taken the most important step of all: investing in myself. It's never too late to take it. I'm living proof of that. Who knows what might happen to you, darling reader, if you give yourself the chance?

CHAPTER 16

A WITW?! Christmas Miracle

Have you ever had an experience you couldn't explain? Maybe the minute you learned someone died, his favorite song came on the radio. Or an old friend you hadn't thought about in twenty years suddenly popped into your head, and within a day, she called you out of the blue. Or you were hopelessly lost on a dark country road and something forced you to take a back road that brought you right where you wanted to go.

Some might call these examples of a woman's intuition, but I consider them to be supernatural. I've felt God's presence several times in my life, and the story I'm about to tell you is the best of them. Get ready for chills.

Over Super Bowl weekend in 2020, Beth, Tess, and I went to Rosemary Beach, Florida, for the annual girls' weekend, when a bunch of middle-aged women get together to chat and eat and put our feet in the pool. Tess was turning twenty-one that weekend, and she would rather hang out with a bunch of old ladies than her friends (or so she said). We had a ball.

In high spirits, we boarded our flights to head home. We

landed in Atlanta to transfer to Knoxville, and I checked my phone. I had a bunch of voicemails from Chuck, Daddy, and my brother-in-law. As soon as I saw that, my heart sank. I knew something terrible had happened. I called Chuck, and he told me that my mama, then seventy-six, had had a stroke.

"Is she going to be okay?" I asked, already sobbing.

He paused. "We don't know. Just get here as soon as you can. She's at Vanderbilt."

I told Tess and she started sobbing.

I could not stand the idea of my mama in pain or of losing her. Maggie and Tess always say to me, "You're not going to die, Mom. We're going to freeze your body. We can't be without you." I feel that way about Lucille. She's been my cheerleader, the love of my life, my best friend. If she wasn't going to make it—a horror I could barely contemplate—I just had to see her one last time.

Hysterical, I explained what was happening to the Delta flight attendants. They started crying too. They came back to us with a big bag. "We're just so sorry and we didn't know what to do. Take this." I peeked inside. It was full of little bottles of wine and champagne from the drinks trolley.

"Thank you," I said. Tess and I sat there, holding the bag of airplane alcohol and crying.

Thank God they were able to change our destination to Nashville. The entire flight was agony. Tess was as distraught as I was. I thought Mama would be gone before we landed. I remember praying, *Can she just be alive for me to see her one more time?*

We rushed to Vanderbilt University Medical Center. Mama was alive, but she wasn't doing well. Daddy told us what happened. She woke up in the middle of the night, nauseated and flushed, her face red as a beet. He went to call 911, and Lucille said, "Jim, don't call the ambulance. I'm ready to go."

Daddy called for an ambulance anyway, against her wishes. She knew she was having a stroke. She also knew stroke victims often lost the ability to walk, or worse. She didn't want to live like that.

Her instincts were correct. She had an ischemic stroke in the back of her neck that cut off blood to the brain. Surgeons operated on the back of her head immediately, and that stopped the stroke. When I was let into her room, I could tell she was still angry at Daddy. She had a tube in her mouth, but when they took that out, she said to me, "I told Jim I was ready. I know where I'm going. And I'm okay with it." She meant heaven. My mom is very spiritual and does not fear death. "I don't want to leave you all, but I miss my parents," she said. "I'm at peace with going." It wasn't the time to argue with her.

She came home shortly after surgery to recover. And she was doing okay. They had her use a walker, and she was moving really well, almost at a little jog. We had to say, "Slow down Lucille!" Her speech and vision were clear. We had hope that she was going to be fine.

But then fluid started pooling in the back of her brain, and they had to operate on her again. Mama was never the same. She came out of that surgery with quadruple vision, which meant she couldn't read. Her balance was off, and that made her vomit. Walking was impossible, so she had to stay in bed or use a wheelchair to get to the kitchen or bathroom. She had to have a feeding tube put in her stomach because she couldn't swallow. To control the drooling, she needed Botox injections in her face. They kept her in the hospital for weeks. It seemed like every day, something else went wrong. It was heartbreaking to watch her go through this. And not once did Lucille complain. She still hasn't. It's been five years.

As I write this, I realize this chapter is a lot different from the others. I don't think anyone would call it a laugh fest. When we were in the thick of this crisis, no one was doing much laughing or anything but worrying desperately about Lucille and Jimmy. We were all miserable and freaked out, and I wouldn't want to sugarcoat the experience of those early days after Mom's stroke. But keep reading. I promise there's a payoff at the end.

Mama was released from the hospital right when Covid-19 shut down the world. The pandemic dominated the news, but for us, Mama's stroke, and our family's new normal, were all we could think about.

My one-hundred-city tour was the biggest thing that ever happened to me, and it had to be postponed because of Covid. Getting that call gave me flashbacks to when my TV show was canceled, but at least this time, I had reason to hope that when theaters opened again, the tour would happen. A small part of me grieved about the tour. A much larger part of me was thankful the pandemic allowed me to help my parents when they needed me the most.

I drove back and forth from Knoxville to Adams to spend several nights a week with them, cooking and cleaning and keeping them company. Beth managed Mom's home care workers. Our kids pitched in with chores around the house. We'd never dealt with anything this big before. And when things had gone wrong, Mama had always been the strong one. Her whole life, she'd been doing for everyone else. Of all the people in the world, she was the last one to deserve a catastrophic illness like this.

In October 2020, my entire family got Covid. It wasn't a walk in the park, but it wasn't horrible. We had a fever and backaches. I couldn't taste or smell, but I could have eaten a horse anyway. You'd think I could diet with Covid, but I was as hungry as ever.

The worst part was being separated from Mama for a couple of weeks. Daddy was angry at me for getting infected. "How could you be so careless?" he asked.

I said, "Lord, Daddy, we weren't out honky-tonking." Who knows how we got it? Tennessee had opened by then. Chuck went to work every day. The kids had to go to their respective jobs. We took precautions and tried not to get infected, but one little molecule snuck in anyway. It was all so upsetting, and Daddy, at eighty, was mentally and emotionally drained from taking care of Mama. As soon as I tested negative and was cleared by my nurse practitioner, I was back in Adams, helping out as much as I could.

The hits kept coming. In December, Mama had a vicious and painful attack. The way Daddy described it, she sat up in bed, vomited, and aspirated the vomit, meaning some of it went down in her lungs. While Mama was struggling to breathe, Daddy called an ambulance in hysterics.

The ambulance took her to a little regional hospital in Springfield. Once she got there and was tested and diagnosed, a doctor came to tell us what was going on. "Her gallbladder is black," he said. "Ordinarily, we'd just take it out. But she's not in any kind of shape to have surgery. We're going to try to heal it from within."

But keeping her in the hospital to heal set off more emotional fireworks. Back then, hospitals were full of Covid patients, and they wouldn't let family members inside if they were at risk for the virus. Dad was terrified about Mom being alone in there. Can you imagine how horrible it would have been for her? Mama's speech was so bad from her stroke that communication was nearly impossible. If she needed anything, none of the doctors or nurses would know how to help her. Daddy wasn't allowed in the hospital because of his age. My sister's husband was immunocompromised, so she couldn't risk it. I was the only one left, and the sweet people at the hospital were okay with my being there because I'd had Covid two months before.

I said to Daddy, "So, my having Covid was actually a good thing. A God thing. I have immunity. Now I can stay with Mama in her room." We were all grasping to find something (anything) positive in this nightmare, so I seized on that idea. And I really believed it.

Daddy was so grateful someone would be at her side and could translate for her. I was one of the few people who understood everything she said. Lucille and I have a strong bond. I know her like the back of my hand. Mom's speech problems had nothing to do with her mental capacity. She was still sharp as a tack. If she had something to say, it was worth hearing. I would look at her eyes, read her lips, and figure it out. And then I would tell the nurses what she needed.

I stayed with her in the hospital room for two weeks, leaving every few days just to shower and change my clothes. I slept on a chair that reclined, but it didn't lock into position. I had to keep my legs straight or it'd fold back up. Plus, it was hard as a rock. I needed physical therapy for several months after sleeping in that chair, but I would do it a hundred times over to be with Mama. We had a ball. We laughed and laughed and laughed. We watched TV, talked (mainly me), and played cards.

She beat me every time. It was a very special time with her. I'm not saying either of us was happy to be there, but we had each other. I think we were both anxious about what was going to happen when she left.

My sister and Daddy visited her once when it was allowed, masked up and socially distanced. If we'd been at a bigger hospital, even that wouldn't have been permitted. I really felt terrible for all those people in hospitals where they weren't allowed to see their loved ones. If Mama had been moved into a nursing home when her gallbladder attack happened, we might not have seen her throughout her whole stay.

A week into that hospital stay, she started coughing frantically and turned bright red. In a panic, I ran to get help at the nurses' station. The head nurse checked her and immediately called a Code Blue. Everybody rushed in. She couldn't breathe and was in terrible pain. They thought she was dying. I had never been so terrified in my entire life. They gave her oxygen and got her breathing under control. Next, they put her feeding tube back in because they thought she might be swallowing food the wrong way. She was put on a liquids-only diet and some medications.

Honestly, I wasn't sure how much more of this I, or my family, could take. We had to find the strength to keep her and Daddy going.

Christmas was fast approaching. We couldn't have a normal holiday that year, or even a nice family dinner. Beth and I had been squabbling about what our roles were in caring for our parents and weren't feeling much good tidings for each other. Daddy was succumbing to stress big time and turned his anxiety into complaining. Honestly, we weren't getting along well.

One night, Beth came by the hospital to drop off something

for Mama. I met her and Daddy in the hospital parking lot. The three of us stood there talking for a few minutes. We were all numb, just going through the motions.

All of a sudden, a little blond woman drove up to where we were standing. She parked and got out of her car. Pointing at the night sky, she said, "That's the Christmas Star. This is one of the few places you can see it. It's shining right over the hospital." I got the impression the woman drove there just to look at it.

Beth, Daddy, and I looked up and saw that one star was shining more brightly than the others. I googled it later. The Star of Bethlehem was visible on that night for the first time in eight hundred years. I gazed up at it, marveling at its radiance. A peace came over me suddenly. From the time I was a child, the story of Jesus's birth has always meant so much to me.

We were all so torn up and worried about Mama. My sister and I were dealing with the tension that siblings go through when a parent is sick and they don't always agree about how to take care of her. My father was just overwhelmed and scared to death. And then this angel appeared and told us to look up. I saw that star and knew God was with us.

No more than ten seconds had gone by since that little woman told us about the star. I looked back down to thank her for pointing it out . . . but she was gone.

Not a trace of her or her car. The space she'd just been in was empty. The three of us were the only people out there. If she'd driven away, we would have heard and seen it.

What in the world? I said, "Where'd she go?"

Beth and Daddy were as baffled as I was. There was no movement anywhere in the parking lot. She had vanished into thin air.

I believe God sent that little woman—maybe an angel in

disguise—because my family was in such a deep hole. We needed to climb out of it for Mama's sake and our own. Looking up at that special bright star gave me the hope I needed to go on. I'm not sure whether Beth and Daddy remember that woman or seeing the star. But I will never, ever forget it.

In that moment, even though I was so sad Lucille had to go through this ordeal, a peace came over me. I felt in my heart the message she'd been saying to me for decades: "It's going to be all right." I just had to surrender and know that God would take care of it. I was going to do the best I could for her and my own family during the crisis. And I did, through future hospitalizations and major adjustments, like installing a wheelchair ramp and a chair lift and finding home care. But I never felt alone.

We weren't alone. God was with us.

Everything's Going to Be All Right

During lockdown, we were all stuck at home. Nobody could go anywhere or do anything. So everyone hung out online.

Me too. I'd go out on the back porch and make videos of me talking about recipes because I love to cook. Mama could eat only pureed foods, so I talked about making her casseroles and Jell-O salads, like the ones I grew up eating at church suppers. Mama loves a Jell-O salad. Apparently, other people do too. These videos got a lot of views! Everyone was home cooking, and they wanted something good to eat.

At the end of the videos, I always said, "Everything's going to be all right." In my heart, I really felt like that was true. *We will open back up. We're not all going to die in the street. Everything is going to be all right.*

I've never felt like my voice was comforting, but it must have been. People who saw my videos started commenting, "I feel better when I hear you say that." Even Reese Witherspoon messaged me and said, "You're doing a good thing, Leanne. Keep going."

Beyond recipes, I talked about taking care of my elderly parents, how my thyroid was doing, and other things people my age related to. I didn't have any makeup on, and viewers liked that. I think they were sick to death of videos of people with filters on their face and perfect lighting. Who needed that? We were all freaked out and sad and worried. People just wanted the truth.

But the truth wasn't always true back then. Remember when they said plastic bags might have Covid on them and we shouldn't bring them into our houses? My daddy would sit and watch the news all day, and it would scare him to death. If the next segment said plastic bags might *not* kill you, Daddy didn't hear that part. He was already freaking out and rubbing down the groceries with Clorox. So I changed my tagline to "Don't watch the news, and everything's going to be all right."

More and more people started following me. They were just everyday people out in the middle of the United States who were trying to find something good to cook and a little hope. They had kids, husbands, older parents. They were going through menopause. And they didn't have a lot of people like them talking to them about what they were going through.

Precious people from North Dakota and Nebraska started sharing their Jell-O salad recipes with me on Facebook. I didn't know they made Jell-O salad in the Midwest. I thought it was just a southern thing. They sent recipes for casseroles and other soft things Mama could eat. And then they started sending Lucille gifts and little things for my grandson, C.W. They were praying for Mama too.

By the end, these videos weren't about comedy anymore. It was much bigger than that.

I thought that I'd feel isolated during Covid and that my comedy career, which was just getting going, would come to a full stop again. But by doing those videos, my community just grew and grew. It came from love. It happened because we were all in this together. It made me feel connected to post about Mama going to a speech therapist or about helping Daddy clorox groceries. And it made this new community feel connected to send recipes and to hear me say, "Everything's going to be all right."

CHAPTER 17

Behind Every Successful Woman Is a Man in Shock

When you've been married for a hundred years, you don't expect things to change. You both have your roles, and they've been hammered out over the decades. It's easy to stay in those roles as long as nothing outside the marriage changes. But if something does, and the marriage doesn't change with it, you're in deep doo-doo.

Remember how I said new couples should have premarital counseling so they're in sync when they get married? It'd also be a great idea to check back in and have postmarital counseling after you've been married for thirty years. At the very least, you can sort through your changing relationship by asking each other some new questions, like:

"Who's in Charge Here?"
My answer: "I want to have an equal partnership, like my mama and daddy."

Chuck's answer: "Me."

Chuck is a man who likes to be in control of himself and the situation. So when I started to get a little famous at fifty-five, my poor husband was completely thrown sideways. For most of our lives together, I'd had to adapt to his way of thinking. But in the last few years, he's had to adapt to mine. And let me tell you, it was not easy for him to give up control.

We all know men have fragile egos, and for some reason, my success wounded his.

When I told Chuck Morgan about my first fifty-city tour, he said, "Wow, good for you." He didn't seem excited; then again, he never showed much excitement. We could go to the nicest steak house in the state, and I'd say, "That meal was incredible." Chuck would reply, "It was okay." I don't think I've ever heard him say, "Oh gosh, that was the best meal I've ever had!" Whereas I say that about three times a week. We have a Grand Canyon–size enthusiasm gap between us, and I sometimes get so annoyed with him I'd like to throw him over a cliff.

When they added another fifty cities to my tour, he was just dumbfounded. I was making a lot of money. He was shocked by it all. And he was not nearly as happy about it as I wanted him to be.

Granted, in terms of marital problems, his not being ecstatic about my tour wasn't that big a deal. It could have been a lot worse. Back in my early twenties, I was in the wedding of one of my oldest friends. She got pregnant and rushed into it. I thought their kooky, new age, hippie ceremony was too kumbaya to be legal. The Unitarian officiant didn't bother with the "in sickness and in health" part. She just said, "Do you dig him? Do you dig her? If you keep digging each other, great. If you stop digging each other, that's that." Afterward, we were having a cigarette behind a dumpster and I said, "I don't think you're really married. You can get out of this thing. I'll help you raise this baby." She gave me a look that said, *Riiight*. She knew she couldn't count on me. I was a wreck at the time. We both were. She told me years later that during her wedding reception, her groom's car was being repossessed. She was too embarrassed to tell anyone that she married a con artist. He was like someone on *Dateline* who you couldn't trust as far as you could spit.

Chuck was raised in the Stone Age school of gender roles. The man made the decisions, and the woman went along with whatever the man did. And for a long time, I was his willing Wilma.

For thirty years, he was in charge, and I was okay with it. But times had changed. I'd changed. I was in the position now to make big decisions—like going on a tour that would take me away from home for weeks at a time—and that was uncomfortable for him. But instead of telling me he felt weird, he just sulked, more silent than ever, if that's even possible.

Despite all this change, some things stayed the same.

"How Are We Going to Spend Our Money?"

My answer: "However we want! Woo-hoo!"

His answer: "We're not buying anything."

My husband had been saving for our retirement since he was twenty-six years old. As frugal as he was (is), he always gave me beautiful gifts for my birthday and Christmas. We shopped at T.J.Maxx and drove old cars, but we sent our kids to private school and got them through college debt free. I have always been proud of Chuck for living up to his promise to take care of me and the kids and give us a good life.

But at some point, you can loosen up.

I had a gig at the Wynn Las Vegas—a huge venue, a dream for me—and we got to the hotel too late to go to the restaurant for dinner. So I ordered room service for us.

Chuck said, "You're going to have room service?" He would

never do that. Whenever we went out to dinner when the kids were little, he told them, "No one gets a Coke. Everyone gets water." I really wished he were able to appreciate and enjoy himself for a change, especially considering my newfound success. It's okay for us to have a cheeseburger and fries sent to the room—with as many Diet Cokes as we want.

I've got to tell you, it felt great to be independent and to bring in money for us, but I was also thankful I could take pressure off Chuck. Apparently, though, he would rather keep the pressure on himself—and on me. We started to have some bizarre discussions about money now that I had some. He thought I'd be irresponsible with it. Maybe that would have been true if I'd suddenly come into money at thirty. I get it. I probably would have bought a llama farm. But I was fifty-five during my first big tour. I'd been through a lot of hard times, and I'd never used wild spending as a coping mechanism, like friends of mine who had separate rooms in their houses for all their Amazon delivery boxes. I had no intention of changing our lifestyle or buying a G-Wagon or tottering around in Louboutin heels.

I had to buy some new dresses, makeup, and hair stuff because, good Lord, I was performing in beautiful theaters across the United States and I wanted to look like somebody! The only reason I upgraded my luggage was because the zipper broke on the ancient suitcase I'd dragged all over the country for two years. I'm sure Chuck would have been happier if I'd kept that suitcase and held it together with duct tape.

I did get my new suitcase at T.J.Maxx. Chuck has rubbed off on me. I do love a discount.

"Are We Having Fun Yet?"
My answer: "Yeah, baby! That's the whole point of life!"
His answer: "Fun makes me nervous."

All his life, Chuck has struggled to relax. I think God steered us together so I would teach him that it was okay to have fun and enjoy things.

Either I was a bad teacher or Chuck was a lousy student. He was stuck in this mindset that if something wasn't hard to do, it wasn't worth doing. And I was coming from a place of "Let's have a good time! Let's celebrate our good fortune!"

But he just couldn't let go.

When I started talking about buying some things that would bring joy into all our lives, Chuck was not really on board. We had so many beautiful memories of that lake house we shared with those other couples when the kids were little. I brought up the idea of giving our grandbabies fun summers like we did for our children.

"Chuck, I'd like to have something on the water again," I said. "We could build or buy a small ranch or a fixer-upper. It'll be fun for the whole family!"

"We can't do that," he said.

"We can! My tour will bring in—"

"We need to see where this is going," he said, meaning my career could come crashing down at any second. When he said things like that, it made me paranoid and upset, like he might be right. Impostor syndrome was bad enough in my head. I didn't need my husband to agree with it out loud. That was the opposite of a good time.

Look, I only wanted three things:

A lake house so I could look at water again while I drank my coffee.

A camper so I could take my grandbabies on some road trips in the Smoky Mountains.

A pontoon with shade so we could ride around the lake and

my grandson, who has some red in his hair, wouldn't get sunburned.

"And that's it," I said to Chuck. "A lake house, a camper, and a pontoon."

"We don't need to spend that money," he said.

To him, money we could spend on fun was better left in a retirement account. Chuck doesn't want or need much. He's never cared what other people have or compared himself to anyone. I didn't object to that. But try as I might, I could not get him to loosen up enough to spend a little on something wonderful for the family.

I'm still working on that.

"Are You Coming to Bed?"

My answer: "Yes, but don't get any ideas."

His answer: [Nostrils flare.]

I remember our early days, when I still had hormones and was excited to make out in a car. I wish I still felt that way. I could get a new purse out of that.

If I said to my husband, "Chuck, suck my neck, as hard as you can, until you put a bruise on me," I think he would have a heart attack from shock. But he'd do it.

I'm in menopause, with no estrogen, no progesterone, and no testosterone. It can make you pretty bitter and angry and not too cute doing you know what! Usually, I wear these loose old gowns to bed because I know I'm going to be hot. Sometimes, I put on a cute little cotton gown that I got at Target. When Chuck sees me in that, his nostrils go crazy. There's no telling what's going to trigger him.

Our dynamic is not as bad as it used to be. Chuck's testosterone has dipped a little. Praise God.

Menopause disrupts my sleep terribly. I haven't slept in years. In desperation, I called my nurse practitioner and said, "Help me."

She said, "Do you want some Ambien?"

"I would love some Ambien. But will I get hooked on dope?"

"I mean, maybe," she said.

I wasn't willing to risk it. She had my compound pharmacist make me a natural supplement with melatonin and passionflower and who knows what else. I keep it by the bed in a pill bottle.

If Chuck comes into our bedroom flaring his nostrils at me, I tell him, "Yes, we can do it. But just know that if you hear that pill bottle shake, it means I've taken a pill. And you've got less than twenty minutes before my eyes roll back in my head. And then I'm going to need you to leave me alone."

He says, "Okay." And then he gets hyperfocused on his phone, looking at sports or something. I'm on my side with two beagles by my legs, praying to the dear Lord, *Please, let me sleep through the night. Lord, please.* I drift off, dead to the world . . . and that's when Chuck remembers me.

He reaches over and grabs one of my breasts. And that puts me into a blind rage.

When he does that, I don't feel bad for forcing him to sleep in a frigid room. I turn the thermostat down to sixty-five degrees. It has to be cold because I have hot flashes and want to live through the night. He would rather it be in the seventies, but I beat him down until he gives in. I know he's uncomfortable. He sometimes wears a golf pullover to bed.

Chuck has always been a night owl and stays up half the night (shivering), keeping me awake when I need to get up early to travel to a show. My nurse practitioner warned me that sleep deprivation is a serious issue and that I have to get enough rest to tour. "Leanne, you may need to have separate bedrooms," she said. "You'll get more sleep, feel better, and be in such a better mood. Tell him you'll have more sex with him too."

Like he'd believe that!

"How Do You Feel?"

My answer: "I feel frustrated that you still don't tell me how you feel!"

His answer: "I still don't understand the question."

It's been thirty years, and I'm still waiting for Chuck to talk about his emotions. Men can only do what they can do. God made them a certain way. They don't have to talk things out, and maybe we don't really want them to.

Now, my little daddy was always very emotional, very quick to cry. I'd get on the phone with him and Mom and I'd tell them something sweet or happy, and all of a sudden, he'd stop talking. I'd say, "Daddy? You still there?"

Mom would say, "Oh, honey, your daddy had to go to the bathroom. He's crying." And then she'd ask, "What'd you cook for supper?" My tender-hearted father's crying fits were just a normal thing.

Again, I'm not saying I wanted Chuck to sob in the bathroom. But some emotion would have been okay. I didn't think he'd ever change when it came to expressing himself.

One night recently, before a very early travel day, I snuck out of our room. Chuck was snoring big, and I slept in Maggie's bed. In the morning, Chuck woke up to see me off. He acted a bit strange, even quieter than usual, which was really saying a lot.

He walked me out to the driveway to say goodbye. I said, "I'll be back home in a week, but I'll call you when the plane lands."

"You don't need me anymore," he said, looking straight ahead, blank expression, just like always. His tone was matter-of-fact, exactly the same as if he'd said, "We're out of eggs." But the words were earth-shattering, all the same.

What in the world? I was dumbfounded. Did Chuck Morgan just open up and tell me his feelings? That he was scared and lonely and sad for himself? Did all his joy stealing and snide remarks about room service come down to his feeling vulnerable in our marriage?

When he showed his truth to me that day in the driveway, it was like currency. It bought more patience with him. We'd been the same way for so long; I had to give him at least a while longer to accept the change in me and in our relationship.

I said, "I still need you, you big ding-dong."

When I got back from that tour, he started asking me my opinion about our investments, as in, "Should we buy some farmland?" He consulted with me about how much we should pay for a new roof. I didn't really know what to say, but I was glad he asked. Once he cracked open his heart, just a bit, our marriage started to become the equal partnership I'd always wanted.

I see a lake house in our future. And a pontoon. I'll compromise on the camper.

CHAPTER 18

The Greatest WITW?! Experience Yet

We all have ideas about what's going to make us feel happy and fulfilled. For most people, I think it's things like getting a great job, buying your dream house, marrying your soulmate, or having children.

For years when the kids were little, the one thing that would have made me feel happy and fulfilled was having a house with working toilets. At least one toilet in our home was always broken. Chuck always said, "There's nothing wrong with them." But I spent half my life jiggling the handles. When I hit it big as a comedian, my first thought was, *Now I can replace those toilets. Now I can pay someone to pull up the rotten shrubs under the porch. Now I can buy a nifty outdoor mini-refrigerator and put little drinks in it.*

Let me just say, the thing that has made me really and truly happy and fulfilled isn't on that list. It didn't have to do with my videos going viral or performing at the Grand Ole Opry or watching my own Netflix special (although that was pretty awesome).

The best thing that has ever happened to me was becoming a grandmother.

Chuck and I found out that our son's wife, Mary, was pregnant in the most darling, precious, from-heaven way. The whole family was at our house for dinner. At the end of the meal, Charlie and Mary gave wrapped boxes to Chuck and me and told us to open them. I tore through the wrapping and found a coffee mug with the word "Grandma" on it. Chuck's said, "Grandpa."

I broke down and cried. They'd been married for four years by then, and we had been trying not to torment them by asking, "So when are y'all going to have a baby?" Then they told us it was happening in such a cute way that I just bawled my eyes out.

When my boy and his wife found out they were expecting, they said things like, "Our baby."

Chuck and I said, "Our baby."

And then they started using words like "boundaries."

I just smiled, kept my mouth shut, and thought to myself, *They don't know what's about to hit them.* They were going to have this precious baby and be up all night for weeks and months, trying to do it all themselves. Then my little daughter-in-law was going to start hallucinating and waking up in the night breastfeeding the lamp—just like I did. And then we'd see who's got boundaries.

My grandbaby C.W. was born in the middle of Covid. Charlie was allowed into the delivery room with Mary, but only him. Mary was heartbroken that her mama couldn't be there to hold a leg. Her delivery was easy, and the three of them came home the next day. And we were right there to greet them.

Well, I was right about the boundaries thing.

When you have your first baby, it's like you're in a war zone.

Constant chaos, stinky diapers, projectile vomiting—it's a mess. After two months of doo-doo bombing on no sleep, they realized they needed help. Charlie called me and said, "Mom, what are y'all doing? Where are y'all? Can y'all come over here? Can we come over there? Can we drop C.W. off so we can take a nap?"

They don't even call us anymore. They just drop that little baby off in the yard. We get him anytime we want him. And we want him *all the time.*

My husband is even worse than I am. I said to Chuck, "Do you wish we could raise him?"

Chuck said, "I am going to raise him." Chuck's got a brand-new truck, and he keeps a car seat in it at all times. He goes and picks up C.W. at day care. They just let him in and let him take that baby home, and then he begs C.W.'s parents to let him spend the night. We've got a crib. We've got clothing, diapers, sippy cups, cream, everything he could possibly need. I think Chuck would love it if the whole family just moved in with us.

Having a grandchild is the most unbelievable "What in the world?" experience yet. Holding him in my arms brought out a love I'd never felt before. You love your children, of course. But you have to be careful with them so they don't turn out rotten. If my children wanted something, like a toy, and cried for it, I didn't rush to get it for them. I knew they were going to be fine without it for a while. I parented so they wouldn't be spoiled or get used to instant gratification.

But with a grandchild, I'm all about instant gratification. When he's with me, this child will never want for anything. I ordered twenty-five pacifiers online. I have a few in every room of my house so comfort is never far away, because when that baby cries, it feels like someone's stabbing me. Charlie and

Mary are trying to wean him off the pacifier, and it's going to kill me. They want to limit his TV, and I can't stand it. I just let it play as long as he wants. I buy him expensive toys too, even if his legs aren't long enough to press the pedals on his new Bat-mobile.

This is why God did not want grandparents to raise children. We would ruin them, and they would never have to go to school.

When Lucille saw C.W. for the first time, she was instantly in love. She said, "He's so pretty. Where in the world did he come from?" This was the same thing she always said to me and my sister. I'm so grateful Mama is still alive to see this precious baby grow into a toddler.

He is beautiful with blond hair and blue eyes, and his teeth are yummy. We just sit and stare at his thighs. He's stout because he comes from farming people. I just kiss him until he swats me away. When he mows the yard with his bubble mower, we cheer like he's just won gold in the Olympics. This baby eats chicken and steak by the fistful, and we sit there and watch, chanting, "Hercules, Hercules, Hercules." He's just so beautiful.

We now have a second grandson, J.J. He's so happy all the time. He looks just like Chuck Morgan. All the babies I had looked just like him. It's so sweet to have brothers in the family; we haven't had that before. We're hoping for ten more. We are having a ball with these precious babies. I hope I'm their best friend. And that they'll invite me camping. We're going to ride bicycles and cook hot dogs on an open fire. My plastic dinosaur budget is out of control.

And Chuck says, "Just throw money, just throw money. You don't need a camper. You don't know how to camp. You need to rent a camper and see how you—"

"Stop it, Chuck. Just stop it."

I'm so proud of Charlie and Mary. Same thing with Maggie

and Tess. They are all doing so well, I could just burst with pride. It was no sacrifice for me to raise them because look at them now. As much as I wanted to be the next Roseanne or Ray Romano, it meant more to me to be their mother. That was my priority. And if no one ever buys another ticket to my shows again, I'll still have a full life because of my family.

I was told early on I had to choose between motherhood and comedy, but for me, the two have always been intertwined. My comedy career began when Charlie was an infant and I started selling jewelry. It continued through all my kids' childhood and adolescence, when I talked about T-ball, Tess's whore outfit, and Maggie's hatred of my chewing. My children were gold mines of material for my act. When they were all grown up and didn't need me as much, my career took off. And I've been having a ball on tour, never more so than when the kids are there with me.

It'd be impossible not to see how my relationships and career have unfolded as God's plan. What He had in store for me is so much more wonderful than what I'd imagined. A mature woman hitting it big in comedy with three well-adjusted, compassionate kids who are my best friends? It's the best of both worlds. Just today, Maggie called to ask me to take a walk with her. I could just kick my heels.

My mission is to find the blessing in everything. It's a real challenge not to be bitter or resentful about the crap we've all been through. If you can look back with an eye toward figuring out why things played out the way they did, you can only marvel and feel grateful. I look back at betrayals and setbacks, losses and heartbreaks, and I thank God for teaching me what I needed to learn and shifting things around so I could appreciate what eventually came my way. Everything was meant to happen how and when it did. And it was for the best. I kept getting up onstage in my capri pants, trying to connect with people while also managing to be a good daughter, a pretty good mama (I think), and a much better wife than Chuck Morgan deserves (just kidding).

People always say that life is short and you need to grab every opportunity because you could get sick or be hit by a bus tomorrow. But if you're lucky, life is also kind of long. By the time you get to my age, you'll likely have faced some terrible things. If you aren't a butthole to other people and you have faith and patience to just let things unfold, you're going to get to the place you want to be in the fullness of time. As my mom said before, during, and after her stroke, "Everything's going to be all right."

So every time I hear myself saying, "What in the world?" I know something good is going to come out of it, somehow, someday. The life I'm living now tastes like icing on the cake. I never thought I'd be in a movie or write a book. And if my career ended tomorrow, that'd be okay. At the very least, I'd figure out a way to look back at what happened and laugh.

ACKNOWLEDGMENTS

There are so many people I am so grateful to who have helped me along the way to bring this book to life, it may take four more chapters!

I want to thank my team that made this all happen in the first place. Thank you, UTA and Levity, especially Nick Barnes and Albert Lee. You spoke this into existence! Thanks also to Derek Reed and the team at Convergent.

To the Talent Team at Netflix: Thank you for taking a chance on a fifty-eight-year-old grandmama from Tennessee. You've made me feel like one of the cool kids.

Thank you, Val Frankel, you smart thing, for paying attention in school. You know I didn't, and I couldn't have done this without you.

Thank you, Karen (Little K, and I know I'm killing you), and to all my close friends for being sounding boards through this comedy journey of mine and, as Prince said, "This thing called life."

Thank you, yummy Brian Dorfman, for believing I had

something and for all the wonderful advice. You're always right, darn it.

Thank you to my precious family. Thank you for letting me tell our stories and for being patient when I'm up against a deadline on our family vacations. You all are my everything.

Thank you to my little mama and daddy, Lucille and Jimmy, and my sister, Beth, for letting me let my little light shine.

Most of all, thank you, Jesus, for loving me even in my darkest hour. Your protection over me and perfect timing led me to this moment.

ABOUT THE AUTHOR

LEANNE MORGAN is a comedian, actress, writer, producer, wife, mother, and grandmama. Her first Netflix special, *I'm Every Woman,* was one of the most-watched specials on Netflix in 2023. Morgan has been named to the *Forbes* 50 Over 50 list and *Variety*'s 10 Comics to Watch list. When she's not on the road, Morgan loves to be at home in Knoxville, Tennessee, with her husband, three children, two grandbabies, and beagle.

LeanneMorgan.com
Facebook.com/leannemorgancomedy
X: @LeanneComedy
Instagram: @leannemorgancomedy
TikTok: @leannemorgancomedy
YouTube: @LeanneMorganComedy

ABOUT THE TYPE

This book was set in Caslon, a typeface first designed in 1722 by William Caslon (1692–1766). Its widespread use by most English printers in the early eighteenth century soon supplanted the Dutch typefaces that had formerly prevailed. The roman is considered a "workhorse" typeface due to its pleasant, open appearance, while the italic is exceedingly decorative.